GURUS ON LEADERSHIP

MARK A THOMAS

First published March 2006.
Reprinted March 2007
Thorogood Publishing Ltd
10-12 Rivington Street
London EC2A 3DU

Telephone: 020 7749 4748
Fax: 020 7729 6110
Email: info@thorogoodpublishing.co.uk
Web: www.thorogoodpublishing.co.uk

A CIP catalogue record for this book is
available from the British Library.

PB: ISBN 1 85418 351 6

Cover and book designed and typeset in
the UK by Driftdesign

Printed in the UK by Ashford Colour Press

The author

Mark A Thomas
Performance Dynamics Management Consultants

Mark Thomas is an international business consultant, author and speaker specialising in business planning, managing change, human resource management and executive development. Prior to becoming a Senior Partner with Performance Dynamics Management Consultants he worked for several years with Price Waterhouse in London, where he advised on the business and organizational change issues arising out of strategic reviews in both private and public sector organizations. His business and consulting experiences have included major organizational changes including strategic alignments, mergers and acquisitions and restructuring.

His current business activities include strategic change management and the facilitation of business planning and top team events. He regularly designs, leads and facilitates top team sessions on a wide range of business planning issues and initiatives – re-organizations, change programmes and mergers. In addition he manages a whole series of executive leadership and organization development initiatives that support wider organizational change – these include executive leadership and coaching programmes. He is an Associate Faculty member at the Tias Business School in Holland, MCE in Brussels and the Suez Corporate University.

Mark's consulting experience has included working with major multi-national and global corporations such as: Lloyds TSB Asset Management, Motorola, Barclays Capital, ECB, Reuters, Cisco, Sony, HSBC, Sun International, Forte, Coca Cola, Mars, Nestle, Aramex,

Philip Morris, Oxford University Press, C&A, Sara Lee, Shell, Schroders, Union Bank of Switzerland, Alcatel, NCR, American Management Association, Alcoa, Aspect Telecommunications, Autodesk and Logica.

Based in London, Mark works across the globe – he has worked in over 40 different countries, including the United States, Japan, Denmark, Singapore, Australia, UAE, Turkey and Russia. In addition to his consultancy and development work Mark is a frequent conference and seminar speaker on business, organization and human resource issues.

Mark is a Fellow of the UK Chartered Institute of Personnel and Development.

His other book publications include:

- *High Performance Consulting Skills,* Thorogood, 2003

- *Supercharge Your Management Role – Making the Transition to Internal Consultant,* Butterworth Heinemann, 1996

- *Mergers and Acquisitions – Confronting the Organization and People Issues. A special report,* Thorogood, 1997

- *Project Skills,* Butterworth Heinemann, 1998

- *Masters in People Management,* Thorogood, 1997

- *The Shorter MBA,* Thorsens, 1991, second edition, Thorogood, 2004

He can be contacted at www.performancedynamics.org

Contents

Introduction   **1**

How to extract value from this book   2

ONE **A taster of leadership – Where have
all the leaders gone?**   **5**

A cautionary tale for today's times   5

The Enron fallout   6

Scandals everywhere!   8

And so to Europe   10

Positions of excellence diminish very rapidly   13

A leadership crisis?   16

But what about public sector values?   18

A legitimate right to lead versus the 'I/me' agenda   22

Private, public and political –
The problem's everywhere   25

Tools and techniques versus character   30

TWO **The Leadership Gurus**   **33**

John Adair – Action Centred Leadership (ACL)   33

Warren Bennis – 'The Dean of leadership gurus'   39

Robert Blake and Jane Mouton – The grid people   44

Ken Blanchard – The one minute manager   49

David Brent – aka Rickie Gervais –
A modern leadership icon   52

Peter Drucker – Management by objectives   55

Fred Fiedler – The contingency theory man   61

Daniel Goleman – The emotional intelligence (EQ) man   66

Paul Hersey – Situational leadership   70

Manfred Kets de Vries – The psychology of leadership   77

John Kotter – The leader and change   81

James M Kouzes and Barry Posner –
Leadership and followership   89

Nicolo Machiavelli – The Prince   93

Abraham Maslow – The motivation man   97

Douglas McGregor – The theory X and theory Y man (or
carrot and stick approach)   103

David McClelland – Achievement, affiliation
and power motivation   106

Tom Peters – The revolutionary leadership guru   112

WJ Reddin – Three Dimensional Leadership Grid   116

Tannenbaum and Schmidt – The leadership continuum   121

Abraham Zaleznik – Leadership versus management   126

THREE   The leadership tool box   131

Some thoughts on leadership and managing   131

The American Management Association's (AMA)
core competencies of effective executive leaders   150

Leadership skills and personal characteristics –
A useful checklist   154

FOUR   Leadership quotes   157

What some people have had to say about leadership   157

Introduction

What makes a great leader?

Are leaders born or made?

Are there common traits that all leaders possess?

Can anyone become a leader?

How good are our leaders?

In a world where every business and organization is in a permanent state of change, these questions are asked constantly. Yet 'leadership' as a word did not really appear in a dictionary until the late 1800s. Prior to that period of time leaders enjoyed largely inherited power and authority. It was the time of Kings and Tyrants. 'Leadership' as a topic for development and study in the business world only came into real focus with the onset of the industrial era of the early 20th century.

Today the business world is obsessed with leadership. Whilst many people argue about how to define it, organizations in turn spend large devote huge resources in trying to attract and develop it. Certainly all our lives depend on leadership, whether it is for the well being of our organizations or individual and family fortunes through the endeavours of our political leaders.

This book is designed to provide an executive overview of past and current leadership thinking. It seeks to distil the work of some of the world's major thought leaders, many of whom continue to share their knowledge and experience about a complex and fascinating facet of all our lives.

In writing a book of this kind I have had to make many decisions with regard to highlighting and editing aspects of all the authors' works. I hope that I have struck the right balance and that my efforts will encourage further reading of the original sources.

How to extract value from this book

This book has been designed to dip into and to get some introductory knowledge and understanding of the theory of leadership, as well as some practical ideas and approaches. In addition to providing a guide to the major leadership gurus I have also included many quotes, checklists and questionnaires that I hope you might find stimulating or useful.

Use this book as a:

- Quick guide or aide-mémoire for your business, university or MBA studies

- Development tool for promoting your own understanding, awareness and skills as a leader

- Stimulus to deal with real life business or organization leadership challenges – to gain some ideas or to reflect on the subject

- Means to provide some stimulating material for a business or leadership presentation or meeting

- Source to aid your consulting or training and development work – looking for ideas and material

Whatever your need I hope you find the book a useful and practical resource.

Mark A Thomas

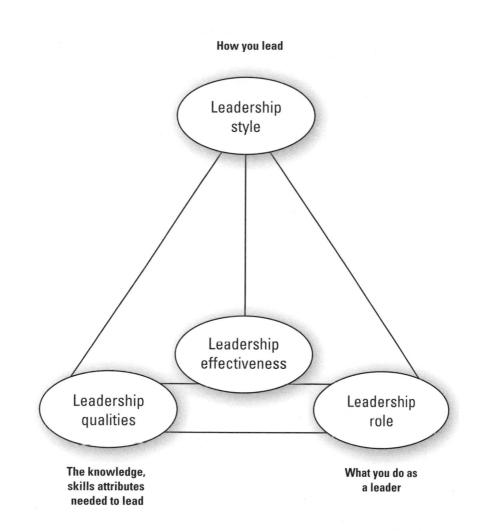

How you lead

Leadership style

Leadership effectiveness

Leadership qualities

Leadership role

The knowledge, skills attributes needed to lead

What you do as a leader

A model of leadership

ONE
A taster of leadership – Where have all the leaders gone?

A cautionary tale for today's times

Are we really getting better? – A personal perspective

> What does leadership mean in today's world?
>
> How well served are we by today's corporate and political leaders?
>
> Does the rhetoric of leadership match the current reality?

This book charts the wisdom and work of some of the world's past and present leadership gurus. It details many of the personal characteristics and traits viewed as critical in leaders. Organizations around the world devote huge resources and spend vast sums of money trying to recruit and develop leaders at all levels. Some of our gurus talk of exciting concepts such as 'transformational leadership' and the 'servant leader'. Some even advise us that in today's organization we are all leaders now. So there is great excitement and energy around the whole leadership field. Our gurus constantly talk of leaders as people who inspire, motivate and stretch mindsets to achieve impossible goals. They create compelling visions and vibrant places to work. But set against the current socio-economic, business environment we ask whether our current leaders are actually making the grade?

The Enron fallout

The Enron corporation scandal of recent years elevated the issue of corporate leadership to the top of the world's business agenda. The collapse of Enron not only devastated the lives of thousands of employees but also resulted in a huge impact on the business world that still reverberates today. Yet it is worth highlighting that only a few years prior to its ignominious collapse Enron was:

- Widely classified as a great corporate citizen

- The winner of six environmental awards

- The year 2000's global 'most admired company'

- For six years listed as 'America's most innovative company'

- Three years listed as 'one of the best companies to work for'

- Praised for its triple bottom-line reports that covered not only economic issues but also its social and environmental performance.

Enron was regularly quoted in business schools around the world as a centre of excellence and a business model for the new millennium. Conference speakers and academics worldwide applauded a new and innovative company that seemed to be writing new rules for the business world. As an asset light company involved in financially linked products and services it was seeking to trade in all kinds of markets. In doing so it developed a highly aggressive internal corporate culture that provided excessive rewards for superior performance. It encouraged an ultra competitive internal market whereby staff were pitted against each other. Yet as a corporate entity Enron collapsed literally in just a few weeks, leaving behind a trail of human and financial destruction. Between 1997 and 2001 Enron's market capitalization grew to an astonishing $50 billion yet it took only ten months for all of that value to be totally destroyed.

The full examination of what went wrong in Enron still continues but what is already clear is that at root of the difficulties was a leadership cadre that seemed to have lost any sense of a moral compass. The high-powered competitive culture that it had done so much to cultivate ultimately created the conditions for its downfall. The result was a dangerous and ultimately fatal belief that Enron's leaders could do anything in order to inflate the financial performance of the company. Enron ultimately became a company that was characterized by lies, arrogance and betrayal.

But Enron is not the only high profile global company to have been dramatically challenged by the role and behaviour of its leaders. Indeed, during the last few years we have seen a number of very high profile companies let down by their leaders. Quickly following on from the Enron debacle was the WorldCom collapse that again saw another major corporate entity ruined by a complex accounting scandal. Whilst WorldCom's chief financial officer Scot Sullivan was being publicly arrested and handcuffed by Federal Marshals, the former Chief Executive, Bernie Ebbers refused to testify in front of the US Congressional Committee investigating a 2001/2 $3.9 billion auditing fraud which involved booking ordinary expenses as capital expenditures.

WorldCom connected some 20 million customers and some of the largest businesses in the world. It was among one of the best performing stocks in the 1990s. In 1998 it acquired MCI in what was then the biggest merger in history. By dressing up the books as they did it enabled WorldCom management to post a $1.4 billion profit in 2001 instead of a loss. In fact WorldCom's market loss fell from $180 billion to less than $8 billion, a far bigger wipe out than was seen with Enron. It also transpired that during his leadership tenure Ebbers had received a $344 million loan from the company.

Scandals everywhere!

Similar financial scandals seemed to be breaking out everywhere and involving companies such as Rite Aid, Tyco, Imclone Systems, Global Crossing and Computer Associates. All seemed to involve not just major financial irregularities but also tales of excessive greed and arrogance by certain leaders. Very quickly all sorts of questions were being raised about the moral and ethical behaviour of these leaders. It appeared that very few seemed to have been worried about their wider responsibilities to staff, company pensioners, investors or customers.

During the period of 1993 and 1996 leaders of Sotheby's in the United States had been jailed and heavily fined for serious offences relating to illegal price fixing in their markets with Christie's. It was alleged that customers were cheated out of $400 million as a result of the agreement to fix commissions and avoid offering discounts. Alfred Taubman the former Chairman of Sotheby's was eventually jailed for a year and fined $7.5 million. Whilst denying any allegations of collusion, former Christie's Chairman Sir Anthony Tennant risks arrest if he travels to the US. Christie's former CEO Christopher Davidge, eventually testified to price fixing in return for immunity against prosecution.

And so events continued to go on. More recently, Rank Xerox faced major US Securities and Exchange Commission investigations into their business affairs. At the same time most of Wall Street's global financial organizations including Lehman Brothers, Goldman Sachs, Bear Stearns, Merrill Lynch, Credit Suisse First Boston, Morgan Stanley, JP Morgan Chase and Deutsche Bank were all under attack for excesses in relation to abuses of clients and customers in the late 1990s and early part of this decade. Elliot Spitzer, the New York attorney general, eventually levied a $1.4 billion fine against 10 investment banks in settlement of the market abuses. In return the banks agreed to make sweeping reforms to settle accusations that their research analysts had misled investors during the 1990s stock market bubble. The settlement resolved multiple investigations into whether banks tried to encourage favour with corporate clients through biased research or offering initial public offering (IPO) shares to executives in hot issues that were coming to the market. This was a practice that became known as spinning. In this huge scandal Jack Grubman, a former star analyst at Citigroup's Salomon Smith Barney, was singled out for particular criticism. He subsequently agreed to a $15 million fine and being banned from the securities industry for life for his role in the debacle. Interestingly Sandy Weill, Citigroup's chairman and chief executive at the time who had asked Grubman to take a 'fresh look' at one of his ratings on AT&T's stock in order to win a lucrative underwriting assignment from AT&T worth $63milion in fees, faced no charges.

But when Sandy Weil was subsequently put forward as a possible director of the New York Stock Exchange Elliot Spitzer went public and commented – "To put Sandy Weil on the board of an exchange as the public's representative is a gross misjudgement of trust and a violation of trust..... He is paying the largest fine in history for perpetrating one of the biggest frauds on the investing public. For him to be proposed as the voice of the public interest is an outrage." Very quickly after this statement Weill withdrew his name from the race.

So intense was the fall-out from these scandals that the debate soon reached the White House and Congress, with President Bush and legislators advocating major change and the need to put corporate responsibility at the top of the political agenda. "We must usher in a new era of integrity in corporate America", argued the President. He went on to argue that "the business pages of American newspapers should not read like a scandal sheet.... Too many corporations seem disconnected from the values of our country". Bush argued that "Corporate America has got to understand that there is a higher calling than trying to fudge the numbers". So great was the threat of these scandals that they seemed to genuinely questioned the integrity of the entire financial system. As Bill Jamieson in *The Scotsman* commented – "A market economy can't function when trust is abused.... When trust is withdrawn, nothing can be rationally priced, for nothing can be taken at face value".

And so to Europe

As these scandals and problems erupted the European business perspective was that it was an essentially US problem. But this somewhat superior view changed very quickly as a series of European scandals came to light. At the time of writing the once revered and globally respected Shell is having its reputation muddied by an over zealous leadership group that falsely booked oil reserves in order to make the company's financial position look more positive. Of course for decades Shell has been held up as an example of business excellence and conservatism. To become a board member of Shell was a signal that you had almost become a statesman in the business world. So it was a great shock to read of former senior executives such as Walter van de Vijver writing emails saying that "*I am becoming sick and tired about lying about the extent of our reserve issues*". The result of this was an overstatement of oil reserves in excess of 4.5 billion barrels which amounted to about 23% of Shell's total reserves. As a consequence of this action the US and UK regulatory authorities levied fines of $150 million against Shell, and Sir Philip Watts former CEO, Judy Boynton Finance Director and Walter van de Vijer all lost their jobs. Shell meanwhile struggles to regain a once revered reputation and has been forced to make radical changes to its management and board structure. The incident has forced some to suggest the once unthinkable – that Shell could be the target of a takeover!

We were also to hear of similar scandals involving other European corporations such as Vivendi where CEO Jean Marie Messier and his huge ego and expansionary ambitions – he spent $50 billion in one year – eventually managed to reduce the company to junk bond status. Edgar Bronfman Jr sold his MCA and Polygram interests to Messier for $34 billion and a 6% stake in the newly formed Vivendi Universal worth at the time $5.4 billion. After Messier had finished his work Bronfman's investment was worth $1billion. As Bronfman later commented, "Unfortunately it is the same old story of power corrupts but absolute power corrupts absolutely". Messier it seemed, developed the view and opinion that he could do no wrong.

Meanwhile in Holland the Ahold Corporation, which was at one time the world's third largest retailer, became embroiled in another financial scandal when it admitted in 2003 that profits in its US subsidiary had been overstated by $500 million. This was enough to send the company into deep crisis and resulted in a clean out of many top executives, including the Chief Executive Cees van der Hoeven and Chief Finance Officer Michael Meurs. Some 50 US executives also left the company and the US Justice Department and Securities and Exchange Commission announced major investigations. As Chief Executive for less than a decade Cees van der Hoeven had built up Ahold by an aggressive acquisition strategy. He was seen very much as the driving force and the dominant personality in the company. But, like some of our other examples, as a leader it is probable that success blinded him to the extent that perhaps he felt he could do no wrong. Today Ahold still struggles to regain investor confidence.

Around the same time as the Ahold scandal broke, Italy witnessed the collapse of one of its most famous companies, Parmalat. Amid allegations of huge corruption involving fraud and cooking the books to hide a $4billion black hole in the accounts, senior members of the founding Tanzi family now sit in Milan jails awaiting trial. As a company that employed 36,000 employees in 126 factories in 30 countries the fall out on investors and staff has been immense, not least to the image of the town of Parma from which Pamalat took its name. The company even took ownership of the Parma football club spending millions to provide international success. But today Calisto Tanzi the 66 year old patriarch of the company appears to have lost everything. His latest claim is that he did not fully appreciate the difficulties that the business was in.

A similar fall from grace also met the once mighty and revered hero of European business Percy Barnevik, who built ABB into a world class business in the 1990s but was forced to make a public apology and return some £37 million of pension arrangements that did not satisfy satisfactory measures of shareholder governance. One Swedish newspaper calculated Barnevik's award was the equivalent to what

7,967 nurses would earn in a year. A once great reputation was ruined with Barnevik having to resign ignominiously as Chairman of Swedish giant Investor and from Astra Zeneca. Shareholders commenting on Barnevik's behaviour argued that, "He has done serious damage to this organization and has flagrantly abused all his trust". Interestingly, previously in his career, Barnevik had strongly supported notions of better corporate governance. At the peak of his powers he was regularly cited in the Harvard Business Review and business magazines around the world as an exemplary leader. For someone whose personal brand as a globally respected leader had flown so high it was again a rather ignominious ending.

The once admired Swedish Skandia financial services group also saw its reputation ruined by the behaviour of some senior executives, including the Chief Executive Lars-Eric Petersen. Skandia had built up a strong international reputation as an innovative and visionary company. At one time it was seen as a brilliant advocate of knowledge management and associated concepts. But it soon failed to cope when booming stock markets fell and it faced major problems in its US businesses. At one time in early 2000 its share price fell by more than 90%. Tied up with this collapse in fortune were allegations of abuse with regard to overly generous stock options, bonuses and perks – most notably apartments in exclusive parts of Stockholm not just for the executives but also their children. Eventually Petersen was forced to leave the company abruptly in 2003. Again, it was a very sad end to what seemed at one point to be a new and vibrant corporate entity that was taking a new direction under an exciting leadership team. But as with Enron we were all left with bitter disappointment.

Positions of excellence diminish very rapidly

But perhaps the most amazing example of all these examples of corporate leadership failure was the figure of David Duncan the Andersen Partner responsible for Enron turning star witness for the US government. Arthur Andersen was without doubt one of the world's greatest corporate success stories for the last 20 years yet it was destroyed in literally a matter of weeks as a result of its relationship with Enron. We still wait to find out the exact details of what went wrong but it is highly probably that the ultra aggressive and driving leadership culture for which the firm was so well known finally caught up with it. There seems little doubt that certain players in the company appeared to have lost their moral compass in pursuit of growth, increased earnings and financial gain. But for a company that was regularly cited as an example of corporate excellence in all aspects of its business model and, rather like Shell, we should perhaps look to learn at how fast a position of excellence can diminish when the leadership compass is lost. Indeed I am a little surprised by how little people have reflected on the collapse of Andersens. Here was a company that was globally recognized and admired for its strategy, financial performance, operational capabilities, branding, and people. Yet within weeks it had disappeared as a corporate entity. The real lessons appear to have been glossed over but what is clear is that some partners in the firm had clearly rejected old values involving integrity and due diligence and replaced them with a belief that revenue growth had to be achieved regardless of any enduring values.

In all it has been estimated that the Directors of US companies worst hit by the market downturn of the last decade cashed in more than $66 billion in shares, prior to the market collapse. Whilst general workers pension funds collapse senior directors are frequently safeguarded by separate schemes that pay out huge guaranteed sums often for a few years service. Such behaviours are adding to a sense that some of our leaders have lost the right to lead. Equally not all these problems can be attributed to the excesses of Wall Street. In recent times as illustrated by the Shell debacle, the UK corporate scene has also witnessed much to cause concern about leadership behaviours. Recall the devastating effect of leaders in companies such as:

- **Mirror Group** – Robert Maxwell stole from his workers pension funds in order to keep his ailing empire afloat. Maxwell was a dominant figure who managed to bully and buy people towards his own way of doing business. Repudiated by many, he nonetheless managed to build up at one stage a huge business empire and enjoy all the trappings of a billionaire only for it to collapse with a devastating impact on employees and pensioners. He eventually committed suicide.

- **Polly Peck** – Asil Nadir fled from the UK authorities in the 1990s as a result of a major financial collapse of his business empire. A rags to riches story, Nadir fled the country in flight of the fraud squad. He became a legendary and high profile leader on the stock market, with some shareholders seeing returns 1,000 times greater than their original investment. But by 1993, Mr Nadir had fled the UK for northern Cyprus as 66 charges of theft involving £34 million hung over him. Like Maxwell, he left behind a huge legacy of disaster for employees and companies. He continues to enjoy a life of luxury abroad and has threatened to return to the UK to clear his name.

- **Marconi** – Lord George Simpson and John Mayo who as chairman and chief executive managed in a matter of a few years to wreck the once great and cash rich company GEC and rebranded it as Marconi – they inherited a company with a £2.6 billion cash pile and left it with a £4.4 billion debt. In the same time they took the share price from £12.50 to 15 pence. Both managed to escape from the company with hugely generous payouts whilst many others struggled to keep their jobs and investments. In fact, Lord Simpson was given a £300,000 'Golden Goodbye' and a reported £2.5 million in pension payments, despite the company's plummeting value. Investors were left with 99% losses at one stage. Today the company still struggles to re-invent itself.

- **Equitable Life** – Formerly led by Roy Ranson and Chris Headdon. The collapse of Equitable Life has left many hardworking and saving policyholders devastated after an aggressive leadership regime that eventually left a gaping £1.5 billion black hole in the company's finances. Ranson was described by Lord Penrose – in a major report on the debacle – as 'autocratic' and 'manipulative'. In the report Ranson was further accused of bullying regulators and failing to keep the board informed about the company's true financial state. Whilst many customers face a harsh and uncertain future Roy Ranson retired on a pension of £150,000 a year. In 1997 he was also paid £314,131 before he retired and was succeeded by Chris Headdon.

- **Marks and Spencer** – Once a legendary business success story Marks and Spencer was eventually brought to a halt by a dictatorial leadership style that was not able to accept disagreement. Whilst Sir Richard Greenbury had overseen some of Marks and Spencer's greatest successes his well documented domineering style meant he ultimately could not accept advice or see the need for change. Eventually he was forced to resign as the company shaped principally by his leadership style moved into a long lasting crisis that is still being played out.

- **British Airways** – Another magnificent business success story that was at one point reduced to a humiliating decline by an inappropriate and insensitive leadership style that eroded the core values of customer service and quality, and saw a major decline in the fortunes of the company between his tenure of 1996 and 2000. Following Robert Ayling's acceptance of the job of Chief Executive, BA shares underperformed the market by 40%. In his first year, Ayling narrowly averted a pilots' strike. In his second year, a three-day strike by cabin crew cost the company £125 million. Low morale at BA is often attributed to the effects of the strike, with Ayling often being the target of ill-feeling among staff. Many would argue his approach severely eroded the successful brand and service ethos that BA once enjoyed to the envy of its competitors.

Whilst each set of circumstances is very different, these corporate examples all raise questions about the behaviour and values of the leaders involved. In so many cases it appears that problems arose because the leaders of these organizations became too powerful and dominant. Their view becomes the only view – the result is that any dissent or disagreement to the leader's perspective is viewed as unacceptable.

It is reported that Sir Richard Greenbury, the former Chairman and Chief Executive of retailer Marks and Spencer had an embroidered cushion in his office that read, "I have many faults but being wrong is not one of them". Whilst Greenbury was enormously successful for many years his autocratic leadership style ultimately caught up with the company. An analysis of his leadership style reveals a focus on making people feel weak rather than strong. Questioning and challenging his decisions was not to be encouraged. As a result important indicators of impending trading and customer difficulties were ignored. In Marks and Spencer's case this leadership approach was to ultimately push the company into a long and dramatic spiral of decline that it is still struggling to overcome. Senior managers refused to challenge Greenbury in meetings. To do so would have resulted in some negative outcome, so they took the easier option and only advised their leader on what they felt he would like to hear. Bad news would be buried before it got to his office. On his store visits managers would be advised in advance not to raise difficult or contentious issues. The end result was an introspective company that failed to see the world around it changing rapidly.

A leadership crisis?

So what does this say about the notion of leadership in a major corporation? Clearly no one gets to lead a major organization without certain qualities. Ambition, determination, single mindedness and a unique sense of business acumen no doubt help the leaders of many business corporations. But many of the recent high profile examples of corporate failure and greed seem to point to failings in more funda-mental leadership behaviours and values. Integrity, fairness and honesty seem to be clearly lacking in many situations. Instead we often see huge egos, the abuse of power, together with selfish behaviours. In some cases there are clear leadership strategies of bullying and intimidation. The result is an emerging crisis of leadership in many organizations; where large numbers of people now hold their leaders in quiet contempt. In the corporate world it seems that naked arro-gance, coupled with extreme ambition and self interest is making for an unattractive notion of leadership. This has sometimes been linked to the so called 'celebrity chief executive'; the belief that a superstar leader can somehow come in and transform a business all on their own. Some of the leaders we have mentioned clearly fall into this cate-gory. They become synonymous with the company and the company's success is solely attributed to them. In contrast when things go wrong such leaders appear all too quick to avoid any kind of responsibility and accountability. Invariably failure is attributed to some other force and it is only after much protest and delay that they are forced to leave or resign.

A closer inspection of the companies we have discussed would reveal that the vast majority of them spend huge sums of money on devel-oping notions of leadership amongst their staff. Many will send their executives to business schools and numerous training programmes on leadership. They will invest heavily in complex processes to iden-tify and develop leadership talent. They will have codes of conduct for every aspect of their business – customers, service, people management and even ethics. So where does this gap between these processes and the reality of leadership behaviour come from? Is it as Edgar Bronfman suggested of Jean Marie Messier, the age old story of absolute power corrupting absolutely? Certainly the leadership examples we have highlighted seem to provide a marked contrast to the words of the many gurus cited elsewhere in this book.

But what about public sector values?

But it is not just in the corporate world that this crisis of leadership resides. The last general election in the UK saw one of the lowest electoral turnouts in our democratic history. This is a dramatic trend that is being repeated across the European democratic process. Many surveys consistently link this worrying trend to the mass apathy that the electorate feel towards politicians and the political process. It is a frightening statistic to learn that more people in the UK voted for the 'Big Brother' television game programme than in the European elections. Many would argue that distrust of politicians is not a new phenomenon but increasingly it seems politicians are viewed as ever more self-serving and remote to the people they govern.

Even in the public sector and civil service, which for so long was felt to value integrity and responsibility, has shown similar problems. In the UK we have witnessed the political scandal associated with the parliamentary standards commissioner Elizabeth Firkin who in 1999 was perhaps over zealous in reviewing some politicians' expense claims and their extra curricula business activities. She had reviewed the activities of certain figures in employing family members and concluded that they had not properly followed the procedures. However, her ruling was rejected by the Members of Parliament on the standards committee. The result was that she experienced great obstacles in trying to operate and soon left her job in circumstances which, she felt, amounted to her being forced out. It was a situation that did not reflect well on our elected representatives.

We have also witnessed the unending posturing of certain politicians, such as the former Transport Minister Stephen Byers who swerved from one political scandal to another whilst denying everything along the way until public pressure forced his resignation in 2002. This was the politician who employed a public relations adviser, Jo Moore, who suggested that events like the New York September 11 tragedy were good situations in which 'to bury' bad government news. Interesting Byers initial stance was to protect his 'trusted' adviser until such time that the sheer force of public pressure and outrage forced her resignation. Couple this behaviour of course with the fall out of the Iraq war and the huge public outcry over the failure of anyone in the UK Government to take responsibility for the failure of the intelligence gathering in the decision to take Britain to war in Iraq. The conclusion after several high profile investigations appears to be everyone was wrong but that no one is responsible or accountable. Perhaps there is no greater decision in life than to take a country to war and for no one to accept responsibility for the terrible set of events surrounding the UK's intervention will remain forever one of the great stains on UK public life.

But it is not just in the messy political and business worlds that problems lie with our leadership cadre. We have also witnessed major scandals in the field of Public Services. The National Health Service has revealed major leadership failings involving the removal of deceased organs without parents or relatives permission. The scandal at Liverpool's Alder Hey Children's Hospital centres on the retention of hearts and organs from hundreds of children. The organs were stripped without parental permission from babies who died at the hospital between 1988-1996. Hospital staff also kept and stored 400 foetuses collected from hospitals around the north west of England.

An official report into the removal of body parts at Alder Hey Hospital revealed that more than 100,000 organs were stored, many without permission. Professor van Velzen who was largely responsible for removing the organs was suspended by the General Medical Council amid fury and protest from relatives of the dead. Professor van Velzen, subsequently blamed the hospital's management for failing to explain to parents what would happen to their children's bodies. Acting chief executive of the hospital, Tony Bell, said he was "deeply sorry" for the hospital's actions over a four year period, but added that pathologist Professor Dick van Velzen must now explain his comments. Again it seemed a case where leaders were not standing up to do the right thing. The findings of an inquiry into the affair were described by the then Health Secretary Alan Milburn as 'grotesque' and telephone help-lines had to be set up to deal with calls from distressed parents trying to find out if their deceased children had been caught up in the scandal.

At the same time the Bristol Infirmary children's heart surgery scandal revealed that sick children and babies continued to be operated on when evidence suggested the operations were extremely dangerous and should not have been undertaken on many occasions. One earlier whistleblower, a Dr Stephen Bolsin, claimed his career was under threat following his attempts to take action with the senior executives and surgeons involved. He subsequently resigned in 1995 and went to live and work in Australia.

James Wisheart and Janardan Dhasmana, two of the key surgeons involved, had by 1997, following further complaints, stopped operating and eventually, after pressure from parents, the General Medical Council (GMC) launched the longest and most expensive investigation in its history. A little over two years later, both surgeons, and a Dr Roylance the health trust Chief Executive, were found guilty of serious professional misconduct. Roylance and Wisheart were struck off, while Dhasmana was banned from operating on children for three years. He was later sacked by the hospital trust involved. Although Wisheart and Roylance had already retired, keeping their pension rights, and in Wisheart's case, thousands of pounds in a merit award conferred for 'excellent practice'.

The GMC decided that both surgeons should have realized d their results were bad and stopped operating sooner than they did. They were also criticized for misleading parents as to the likely success rates of the operations their children were about to undergo. Despite the evidence all three doctors still insisted they did nothing wrong – or at least did not perform badly enough to merit being punished by the GMC.

Where were the responsible leaders when these problems started to emerge? A key report into the scandal commented that there was a 'club culture' amongst powerful but flawed doctors, with too much power concentrated in too few hands. Dr Stephen Bolsin, the man who is widely credited with blowing the whistle on Bristol claims he was virtually driven out of medicine in the UK after proving the catalyst for the ensuing scandal.

But what made a relatively junior consultant anaesthetist take the extreme step of risking his career in such a manner? He summed up his response as, "In the end I just couldn't go on putting those children to sleep, with their parents present in the anaesthetic room, knowing that it was almost certain to be the last time they would see their sons or daughters alive". Surely, if anything, this was an act of leadership in very tragic circumstances. The subsequent public inquiry resulted in a damning report that concluded that between 30 and 35 children who underwent heart surgery at the Bristol Royal Infirmary between 1991 and 1995 died unnecessarily as a result of sub-standard care.

We also still live with the fall out from the Stephen Lawrence murder inquiry and the vast implications for the role of the police and the law and order agenda. The 18-year-old A-level student was fatally stabbed at a bus stop near his home in Eltham, south-east London in April 1993. A 1997 inquest ruled he had been "unlawfully killed in a completely unprovoked racist attack by five white youths". The original Metropolitan Police investigation which did not lead to any prosecutions was later found by Sir William MacPherson's 1998 major public inquiry to be racist and incompetent. The inquiry became one of the most important moments in the modern history of criminal justice in Britain. Famously concluding that the force was 'institutionally racist', it made 70 recommendations and had an enormous impact on the race relations debate – from criminal justice through to all public authorities.

What remains clear is that past police leaders appear to have been unable to root out unacceptable practices and challenge a very harmful culture within the police service. What do such matters say for the quality of leaders we currently enjoy? Just as with the Wall Street Banks, we know that Police organizations along with other public sector bodies, will spend large amounts of time and resources devoted to the development of leadership behaviours and practices. No doubt police leaders would talk of the importance of leadership and attend conferences on such matters. Yet the reality seemed to fall well short of the day to day reality never mind the desired ambition.

The cynics might of course say that words such as 'honesty' and 'integrity' have in reality little to do with business. After all it is a long time since the phrase 'my word is my bond' was whispered in the City of London or global capital markets. Yet in the public sector we have supposedly highly educated and well-intentioned police leaders, surgeons, doctors and hospital administrators supposedly bound together by an ethic of service and care. So why do these crises seem to be increasing? What has happened or is happening to our concept and quality of leadership? Are simple failures to accept and take responsibility clouding our views of all leaders?

A legitimate right to lead versus the 'I/me' agenda

In reviewing the work of many of the gurus listed in this book it is clear that being a true leader often involves taking tough and demanding decisions that do not always please everyone. But our review also reveals in most cases, that leadership implies having a legitimate right to lead: where values such as integrity and fairness are essential to any leaders make up. Whether you are a Chief Executive, political leader, factory manager or hospital team leader your values are critical. But on the evidence of some of the examples we have examined, it seems a huge gulf has opened up in relation to what leaders now regard as acceptable behaviour. There is little doubt that some business leaders exercise power and patronage as if they were later day emperors. In turn, politicians no longer resign on matters of principle. The suspicion is always that no one will accept responsibility and that denial is always the first line of defence.

My current experience of working across the globe at all levels of business reveals an immense feeling of dissatisfaction with the quality of leadership currently being shown. Most people have no problem with business leaders who are successful and who generate massive, long-term shareholder value. But the frequent perception given is that many corporate leaders are solely concerned with an inherently selfish 'I' and 'Me' agenda. Principally this philosophy is characterized by the desire to inflate their company's share price in the shortest possible time in order to trigger enormous stock options, regardless of the long-term strategic implications. When they screw up they still win generous payoffs and pension payments, yet leave many employees lives devastated. Very few ever express regret or actually admit errors, never mind utter the word 'sorry'!

Just look at some other recent examples of corporate leadership:

- In January 2002 Al Dunlap, former CEO of Sunbeam, was fined $15 million for falsely reporting performance. At the same time he managed to plunge the company into a massive financial crisis from which it seeks to regain credibility. His nickname was Chainsaw Al, based on his previous appetite for enacting massive job cuts in his organizations. Not even Dunlap's harshest critics could have predicted such a disastrous outcome when the chief executive first strode into Sunbeam. The day after Sunbeam announced that it had hired the self-styled turnaround artist and downsizing champion as its CEO, the company's shares soared nearly 60%, to $18.63. At Scott Paper Co., Dunlap's last CEO assignment, he had driven up shares by 225% in 18 months, increasing the company's market value by $6.3 billion.

  In Dunlap's presence, people quaked. Staff feared the verbal abuse that Dunlap could unleash at any moment. As John A Byrne who wrote a book titled Chainsaw reported, "At his worst, he became viciously profane, even violent. Executives said he would throw papers or furniture, bang his hands on his desk and shout so ferociously that a manager's hair would be blown back by the stream of air that rushed from Dunlap's mouth. "Hair spray day" became a code phrase among execs, signifying a potential tantrum. It seems to be another classic example of unbridled power and arrogance facing igno-minious disgrace. But at one time Dunlap was feted as an extraordinary leader by many commentators.

- Sir Ian Vallance, Chairman of BT, led the company into a situation where it was left with a £30 billion debt and was subsequently forced into a £6 billion rights issue to play down the debt. He left BT with a pension of £355K on top of benefits of £30K and additional fees of £321K for 12 months work as Company Emeritus President – a honourary post given to him after he was pushed out as Chairman. At the same time his former Chief Executive Sir Peter Bonfield's saw his pay at BT rise by 130% to £2.53 million. He eventually left the company with £1.5 million in his pocket despite the fact that the company had lost half its market value the previous year.

Despite these clear failures of performance these leaders still argued for their £1 million plus payoffs as part of their contractual arrangements. Legally they may be right but from a simple meritocratic and moral perspective they appear bankrupt. It is what has come to be known as the 'reward for failure' syndrome and has provoked a political debate on both sides of the Atlantic. To some this debate is simply about a few bad apples that always occur in any sphere of life. There is no need to worry and this does no damage to the wider well-being of our organizations and society. To others the problem is symptomatic of a much deeper leadership malaise. As two well-known commentators, Henry Mintzberg and Robert Simons have commented, "A syndrome of selfishness has taken hold of our corporations and our societies, as well as our minds... If capitalism stands only for individualism it will collapse".

Sir Howard Davies, formerly head of the Financial Services Authority (FSA) in the UK, commented that ethics in the City "is a bit of an uphill struggle". He went on to express regret that financial companies who had clearly been guilty of miss-selling mortgages and pensions were reluctant to contact customers after the fact. Again, the heads of these major businesses seemed to show no remorse that their organizations and staff had clearly failed to set out the real implications of the products they were selling to their customers.

In all of this debate it seems that customers, suppliers and staff simply don't figure on the agenda. As a result the leadership perspective is increasingly viewed as one of pure greed and self-interest. As one City analyst pointed out to me when asked how some of the well-known and disastrous acquisitions ever saw the light of day, "You have to understand if you have an aggressive and very ambition CEO who is being encouraged by countless investments bankers to go after an acquisition, in the sure knowledge that it will ramp up revenues and increase the share price in rapid timescales, then nothing on earth is going to stop them!"

Private, public and political –
The problem's everywhere

In the same breath many people will comment that this behaviour mirrors the same problems with our political processes. Politicians who will say anything to get elected only to then renege on their promises once in power. Nothing new here perhaps, but today's 24 hour reporting means that people have the ability to compare and contrast as never before. The end result is a common belief that all politicians seek office purely for their own self interest. This is, of course, a very harsh and unfair judgement on many hardworking and dedicated politicians. But that is one of the consequences of poor leadership, you end up being tainted by your leaders' behaviours. As I write, the UK press are having a field day about the breakdown of the relationship between Tony Blair and Gordon Brown. The two, it seems, cannot stand the sight of each other and constantly allow aides to brief against the other side. Meanwhile they are custodians of two of the great offices of State, yet the behaviour they display appears more appropriate to two rather junior middle managers squabbling over a new job. When of course confronted about the problem both refuse to answer direct questions preferring to speak in coded messages such as, "The real answer is probably yes but I obviously cannot say that on the record". So we speculate that we will all have to wait for their richly rewarded memoirs to read the truth of the relationship and have the suspicions confirmed.

Just as we marvelled at former Enron CEO, Jeffrey Skilling, arguing that as a former Harvard MBA and senior McKinsey partner he did not understand financial matters and was not fully conversant with the complexities of the Enron balance sheet!

Who wants to hire a former Maxwell Finance Director? One of my relatives worked at a company that did and ended up losing thousands of pounds in a scam that had obviously been learnt at one of Maxwell's former companies. The individual and a large sum of cash disappeared from the company.

Who can honestly say that they admire the way in which the former corporate leaders of Equitable Life treated the policyholders and pensioners – people who had saved diligently for years only to see their savings and pensions destroyed? Who indeed feels comfortable buying any financial services product after the pensions and endowment mortgages miss-selling scandals of the '80s and '90s? In fact where were the brilliantly clever actuaries when the sales and marketing directors were reporting record sales of these products? Who registered concerns that perhaps it was not in the best interest of the nurse or redundant miner to switch their pensions or invest in an indemnity product? Indeed, how many corporate leaders from the financial world have been brought to account for this flagrant abuse of customer trust? Many it appears have been allowed to flourish whilst existing customers are expected to pick up the additional costs of repairing the damage and correcting the wrong.

Ask yourself whom do you truly admire and respect as a political leader? Nelson Mandela, perhaps? But ask yourself who is next on your list in today's world?

Who feels that Lord Falconer's persistent inability to ever apologize or offer his resignation over the Millennium Dome fiasco served politicians and their sense of integrity? For that matter, you can of course add Peter Mandelson who was also a major architect of what was clearly an abject failure and a massive waste and abuse of taxpayers' money. Yet both have gone onto far greater roles of power and significance. Lord Falconer after several other top government jobs now wields tremendous power as the current Lord Chancellor yet he has never stood for elected office. A man of undoubted ability but it seems a major element of his success is based on the patronage of his former legal colleague Tony Blair.

Who watched Michael Howard's infamous BBC interview with Jeremy Paxman and felt a sense of pride in the integrity and openness of politicians? Michael Howard, then Home Secretary was questioned on his alleged threat to the Head of the Prison Service. Paxman asked Howard the same simple and straightforward question 17 times, but Howard as a former barrister, still refused to provide a simple yes or no answer. Did he have a sense of shame as to how this might have reflected on his image or that of all politicians? It seems that politicians of all shades now adopt this behaviour. President Clinton is feted by millions as a great leader yet he clearly misled the America people about his behaviour during the Lewinski scandal- but it seems this is OK. Of course some people argue that political leaders are no different to the rest of us in committing indiscretions and that such behaviour is part of life. The real question is whether leaders who pronounce on others have an obligation to at least live up to a sense of honour.

Who warms to Jeremy Paxman's regular BBC Newsnight programme announcement that "whilst we extended an invitation to the Government to talk about this issue we were advised that no one was available to speak to us." Indeed, in the political world our leaders seldom venture out to meet the real public and engage on the real issues. Tony Blair was in shock during the last election when presented with the anger of a woman outside a hospital pleading for a better service for her cancer suffering husband. Equally, as leader he was caught off balance in a BBC television studio by a distraught mother challenging him over donor transplant provision? The fact is our leaders now choose to operate in environments that are very controlled; where people are selected for their ability to show respect and stay on message. It is said that Tony Blair will not be interviewed by the infamous BBC Today radio programme because of the tough and critical questioning stance they take on political issues. The very same sort of problem that perhaps was responsible for the Enron debacle – show respect and deference to authority and you get on, speak out and your career suffers or, in the world of political commentary, you won't get the right access or inside news. In effect it all amounts to the same thing, as a leader we can bully you into submission.

Even more disturbing for the corporate world is how we managed to get here after some 40-50 years of intensive leadership research, development and training. This book will set out some of the ideas of many foremost leadership gurus. You will read about motivating and aligning people and the creation of exciting visions. Couple their words and efforts with the enormous amounts of time and money that have been spent on leadership research and training in organizations. Contrast that with some of the examples we have discussed and ask whether all of this leadership effort has worked? What is it that is causing this disconnect between the reality of leadership in many organizations and what is preached elsewhere? This question poses major challenges for people who shape much of the leadership agenda in organizations. How do human resource and development practitioners see their roles in shaping the true quality of leadership in an organization or business? What is on the priority list of development needs and what exactly is being taught? On what basis are people selected for leadership roles? On present performance do we appear to be wasting our time with all this activity and investment? I recently read an article by a learning and development specialist at Shell extolling the virtues of their leadership development approach – he clearly failed to explain what leadership values had led his senior executives to lie about the value of their oil reserves. As ever it seems there is one rule for the corporate leaders and another for everyone else. Is it that the virtues advocated by many of our gurus are in truth extremely difficult to find? Or is it that we allow negative leadership behaviours to go unchallenged and unchecked? I am not proposing answers to these questions but I do think we need to start debating them as something appears to be going seriously wrong with the quality of leadership.

During the Enron and Wall Street scandals both *The Economist* and *BusinessWeek* magazines sought to address the leadership issue in depth. Yet both failed to address the ethical or character side of the problem. Indeed, in one edition *BusinessWeek* simply devoted a final paragraph to leadership after emphasising the mechanistic roles and responsibilities of the board, accountants, analysts and regulators. Any individual sense of what is essentially right and wrong did not seem to enter into the analysis. *The Economist* similarly understated the position as one of a failing in accounting standards and reporting. At the time of writing, a whole new global industry is being created around new standards of corporate governance. The Sarbanes-Oxley Act of 2002 in the United States has heralded in a new era of corporate and business transparency. Consultants and professional accountancy firms are earning millions in revenues as a result of responding to this new culture of 'corporate governance'. Professional codes of ethics and standards are being created at an enormous rate, yet little debate is being focused on the question of 'character'. It is as if a written code or directive will fix the problem of excessive ego and greed.

Tools and techniques versus character

Perhaps the real problem is that our focus on leadership is centred too much on tools and techniques. Perhaps this mechanistic approach is obscuring our view of what is really required. Whilst competency checklists, so much favoured by major human resource specialists as important perhaps the real focus and debate around leadership needs to shift to the fundamentals. Values such as honesty, integrity, openness, justice, fairness and accountability, require little definition. Yet they seem very remote and alien concepts to some of our leaders in the corporate and political worlds. As someone once said, truth is a matter of conscience not fact. When faced with difficulties too many of our corporate leaders seem to run to their personalized employment contracts and cling to lame excuses instead of accepting their fate with honour. One senior director in a major business recently said to me that he simply could no longer defend his Chairman's huge pay increase when the business had done so badly. One of our key leadership gurus is Warren Bennis and he has commented:

> *"The future has no shelf life. Future leaders will need a passion for continual learning, a refined, discerning ear for the moral and ethical consequences of their actions and an understanding of the purpose of work and human organizations."*

When contrasting this perspective with some of our 'bad' leadership examples we are left wondering what has happened to some of our leaders. Perhaps what we need in today's world, as Bennis suggests, are leaders who are more willing to use their conscience to serve their followers. But that presupposes that some of today's leaders have consciences! As the expression says – the fish rots from the head! The indications are that already the Enron scandal has resulted in a different accounting and reporting landscape but it will not solve the individual question of 'character?'.

Dr Reverend Martin Luther King once said:

"There comes a time in life when one must take a position that is neither safe, nor politic, nor popular, but he must take it because his conscience tells him it is right."

This statement that will no doubt be reverberating down the empty halls of whatever was left of the Enron Corporation headquarters, and many audit firms and corporate boardrooms around the world today. Whilst the full scale of Enron's problems may still take time to unravel, in the end it will come down to a simple test of character, as it always does. Just as President Clinton needed to answer the question so will David Duncan of Andersen. Did you or did you not know that what you were doing was wrong? A simple 'yes' or 'no' answer is all that is required. Despite their brilliance many of our leaders find this question too complex to answer. Be warned, I fear we have not yet seen the worst. Remember some of the corporate leadership examples we have reflected on when you read some of our gurus. The message is clear; we would like a better quality of leader please!

POSTSCRIPT – AND SO IT CONTINUES!!!

As I draft the final stages of this book we are again witnessing in the UK the latest round of emerging leadership crises.

The Rover Car Group

As the Rover Car Company sinks into bankruptcy we discover that the management team of four, led by John Towers who rescued the business from failure some five years ago have managed to build a personal pension pot of some £16.5 million. When BMW originally decided to sell Rover to this management team it did so for the nominal sum of £10 added to which it provided a soft loan of £427 million. In the ensuing five years Rover struggled to build a successful business and has never made a profit. At the time of writing it sadly looks like the company is doomed and that thousands of workers will lose their jobs and pensions. Despite this the management team who appear to have risked very little at the outset of the venture stand to walk away with substantial financial gains. Against this seemingly ludicrous example of meritocracy and equity the government have announced an investigation into the affairs of the company. But whatever the result it is yet again the kind of story that gives corporate leadership an ugly name.

The British Army

For decades the British Army has prided itself on the training of its officer corps. Sandhurst Military Academy has enjoyed a worldwide reputation for growing the civilized officer – a just soldier who is guided by a clear moral code in the seemingly immoral theatre of war. We have been led to believe that in the British Army there was always a clear ethical code of what was deemed acceptable and unacceptable behaviour even in the impossible conditions that they are asked to perform. Yet the organization is currently re-examining its entire leadership approach against a background of proven allegations of abuse in its treatment of new Army recruits and prisoners of war in Iraq. In both cases it seems that there has again been a loss of moral compass with regard to the duty of care exercised by officers over their soldiers and prisoners. The result has been to allow a culture of bullying, harassment and abuse to go unchecked. Again it seems that some leaders were lacking in character and as a result their negligence and behaviour has put a huge stain on what was generally regarded as a centre of excellence.

WorldCom – Update

In March 2005 Bernie Ebbers the former head of WorldCom was found guilty of leading an $11billion accounting fraud that resulted in the largest bankruptcy in US history. He now faces more than 20 years in prison when he is sentenced in June 2005.

TWO
The Leadership Gurus

John Adair – Action Centred Leadership (ACL)

John Adair is one of the very few leadership and management gurus who lives outside of the United States. Born in 1934, he is a highly distinguished academic, consultant and author.

Adair studied history at Cambridge University and holds higher degrees from The Universities of Oxford and London. At the age of 20 he was adjutant of a Bedouin Regiment in the Arab Legion. After Cambridge he became senior lecturer in Military History and Leadership Trainer Adviser at the Royal Military Academy Sandhurst. In addition to consulting with major companies he works with numerous government bodies covering every field from education to health.

He became the world's first Professor of Leadership Studies at the University of Surrey and is regularly cited as one of the world's most influential contributors to leadership development and understanding.

Despite this impressive background John Adair has perhaps not enjoyed the universal success associated with some of the other gurus included in this book. Whether or not he failed to benefit from an aggressive marketing adviser; as is seen with so many of the US based gurus, is not clear. More likely is the observation that John Adair has devoted a lot of his career in helping develop leadership in the education, voluntary and health sectors and seems to have been a person who has given rather more than he has taken. But certainly his contribution to the study of leadership has been immense and is worthy of a much wider audience.

What is he famous for?

Adair's leadership work is written in a hugely rich, detailed and insightful manner that reflects his strong academic interest in both modern and classical history. He draws analogies from many varied sources and his view of leadership role models extends well beyond today's corporate world. With Adair you can expect to learn about leadership from a wide array of history's greats including Napoleon, Lao Tzu, Alexander the Great, Lawrence of Arabia, Gandhi and Charles de Gaulle. More likely to quote Max Weber and Thomas Carlyle than today's luminaries, his work offers many intriguing insights into the nature of leadership. Central to Adair's approach is that leadership skills can be developed but that other qualities such as integrity and humility are essential to the makeup of an effective leader. He has also written other successful works on decision-making, time management and innovation and problem-solving.

Yet despite a huge body of work it is for the 'Action Centred Leadership' (ACL) model that John Adair has become most famous. Originating out of his work in developing young officer cadets at Sandhurst, his model is a simple but elegant guide to the functions of an effective leader. The model was originally developed in the early 1960s and was called Functional Leadership. It was subsequently developed in the 1970s by the Industrial Society and soon became known in the commercial and industrial world as Action Centred Leadership.

The ACL model is represented by three inter-locking circles encompassing the following:

1. Achieving the task

2. Building and maintaining the team

3. Developing the individual

Adair describes leadership as akin to juggling or balancing these three circles or 'balls' in the air at the same time. The power of his model is that it sets out in simple terms the classic tasks that need to be performed by an effective leader. For Adair leadership is all about effectiveness – what you do – rather than who you are. Using his framework allows us to assess our own leadership effectiveness. The three circles overlap as success in one cannot be achieved in isolation to the others. For example, any team that is not task focused will invariably suffer poor working relationships and this will impact on the capability of individuals. So, leaders have to focus on all three dimensions. A leader who is excessively task focused might achieve results in the short-term but if their approach is at the expense of the other dimensions they may well become autocratic. In turn this will generate high levels of staff turnover as individuals become disillusioned with a dogmatic and authoritarian approach.

KEY FUNCTIONS		TASK	TEAM	INDIVIDUAL
COMMUNICATIONS	Define Objectives	Identify task and constraints	Involve team Share commitment	Clarify aims Gain acceptance
	Plan Organize	Establish priorities Check resources Decide	Consult Agree standards Structure	Assess skills Establish targets Delegate
	Inform Confirm	Brief group and check understanding	Answer questions Obtain feedback Encourage ideas and actions	Advise Listen Enthuse
	Support Monitor	Report progress Maintain standards Discipline	Develop suggestions Co-ordinate Reconcile conflict	Assist/Reassure Recognize effort Counsel
	Evaluate	Summerize progress Review objectives Replan if necessary	Recognize success Learn from failure	Assess performance Appraise Guide and train

Adair's Action Centred Leadership can be summarized by the following activities:

1. Set the task(s): Communicate with enthusiasm and detail the task(s) that needs to be accomplished.

2. Make leaders accountable for up to four to fifteen people: Brief and train them in the three leadership dimensions – Task, Team, and Individual.

3. Plan the work, design the roles, check progress and manage any work processes to ensure that you have the commitment of individuals and the team.

4. Set individual targets after discussion and consultation with staff; discuss performance and progress with each team member.

5. Delegate decisions to individuals.

6. Consult early with people who may be impacted by any decisions you make.

7. Communicate the importance of individual roles. Explain decisions fully to help people in implementing them. Brief your team monthly on any new developments, successes, policy changes, people developments or other critical points.

8. Constantly seek to train and develop people.

9. Care for the well-being of team members – improve working conditions or arrangements and deal with any grievances promptly.

10. Monitor all your management actions – learn from successes and mistakes.

11. Practice Managing by Wandering Around (MBWA) and observe, listen and praise people.

12. Remember to have fun and ensure that the team enjoys itself.

ACL Model

1 Achieve The Task	2 Build The Team	3 Develop Individuals
Define tasks	Consult others	Delegate tasks
Check resources	Set out accountabilities	Listen
Set standards	Encourage and support	Coach
Brief the team	Answer questions	Recognize efforts
Check understanding	Ask for and give feedback	Manage performance
Manage time	Co-ordinate all efforts	Train and develop skills

1 Achieve The Task	2 Build The Team	3 Develop Individuals
Report progress	Encourage risk taking	Be flexible
Review objectives	Use humour/fun Learn from failure Celebrate successes	Let go
Manage progress	Resolve conflicts	Encourage
Recognize priorities	Acknowledge successes	Praise successes
Act decisively	Be creative	Counsel

Despite its huge success, by the 1990s the ACL model fell out of fashion. As a leadership model it was never really subjected to the clever marketing, brand management and re-invention that characterizes some of the US based leadership models. Consequently it is viewed by some people as being a slightly out-dated and rather old fashioned model. This is an unfair criticism as the model certainly stands the test of time. With its strong focus on the practical and behavioural side of leadership the model remains as valid today as ever. The focus on effectiveness – *what you do rather than what you are* – is a powerful message for any aspiring manager and leader. Adair provides practical advice on how to begin the process of leading others.

He provides a superb short course in leadership which illustrates some of his philosophy on leadership:

The six most important words for a leader	"I admit I made a mistake"
The five most important words	"I am proud of you"
The four most important words	"What is your opinion"

The three most important words	"If you please"
The two most important words	"Thank you"
The one most important word	"We"
The least most important word	"I"

Adair also talks about the 50:50 Rule:

- 50% of motivation comes from within a person.
- 50% from their environment, especially from the leadership encountered therein.

It is well worth the investment of time to revisit some of Adair's more general leadership works as they provide a refreshing break to today's 'success recipe' approach to leadership.

Essential reading

- *Effective Strategic Leadership*, John Adair, Macmillan, 2002
- *Inspiring Leadership*, John Adair, Thorogood, 2002
- *Great Leaders*, John Adair, Talbot Adair Press, 1999

Warren Bennis – 'The Dean of leadership gurus'

In 1993 a survey conducted by the Wall Street Journal listed Warren Bennis as one of the 10 most sought after speakers on management topics. In 1996, Forbes magazine designated him the 'Dean of leadership gurus'.

He is a University of Southern California (USC) professor and professor of business administration, and founding chairman of the USC's Leadership Institute. He also serves as the chairman of the governing board of the Centre for Public Leadership at Harvard University's Kennedy School and is a distinguished research fellow at the Harvard Business School.

After earning a PhD in economics and social science at the Massachusetts Institute of Technology, Bennis served for several years on the faculty of MIT's Sloan School of Management and succeeded Douglas McGregor as chairman of the Organizational Studies Department. He has also served on the faculty of Boston University. As a university administrator, Bennis is a former provost and Executive Vice President of the State University of New York at Buffalo and was President of the University of Cincinnati from 1971 to 1977.

He is also Visiting Professor of Leadership at the University of Exeter (UK) and a Fellow of the Royal Society of the Arts (UK).

Bennis has consulted for a large number of Fortune 500 companies. He is a founding director of the American Leadership Forum and has served on the national boards of the U.S. Chamber of Commerce and the American Management Association.

In addition to receiving eleven honorary degrees, Bennis was awarded the 1987 Dow Jones Award for 'outstanding contributions to the field of collegiate education for business management'. He has authored over 26 books, including the best-selling *Leaders* and *On Becoming a Leader*, both translated into 21 languages. *The Financial Times* recently designated *Leaders* as one of the top 50 business books of all time.

Despite his increasing age he still spends part of his time in Europe, South America and Asia. He has been the US Professor of Corporations and Society at the Centre de'Etudes Industrielles in Geneva, a professor at IMEDE in Lausanne, the Raoul de Vitry d'Avencourt Professor at INSEAD in Fontainbleau. He is also a founding director of the Indian Institute of Management, Calcutta.

One of Bennis's accomplishments is that aged nineteen he was one of the youngest infantry commanders in World War II and was decorated with the Bronze Star and Purple Heart.

What is he famous for?

"I tend to think of the differences between leaders and managers as the differences between those who master the context and those who surrender to it."

Warren Bennis, as his vastly impressive career resume illustrates, is frequently described as the major leadership guru. Abraham Maslow, himself a major guru once described Bennis as "one of the Olympian minds of our time".

Now into his 70s his great contribution has been to establish a new approach to understanding leadership. Bennis tended to eschew the heroic traditions associated with traditional leadership thinking and the concept of traits. Not for him is the belief that leaders are born. Rather Bennis believes that leaders can be made. Interestingly Bennis was also one of the first people to argue that leadership exists at all levels within an organization and that we need to revise our beliefs that leadership is for the chosen few. In his view leadership is exercised at all levels within an organization. For Bennis real leadership begins with a vision and the ability to see new approaches and opportunities. From this perspective he argues that true leaders go on and inspire others to deliver the vision. He also developed his now classic differentiation between leadership and management:

"Management has to do with efficiency, with making things run properly. Leadership in contrast is concerned with identity – why we are here; what our business is; what our destination, goals and mission are."

Whilst for Bennis there is a profound difference between management and leadership he nonetheless argues that both are of vital importance to organizations. He writes "To manage means to bring about, to accomplish, to have charge of or responsibility for, to conduct." Whereas "Leading is influencing, guiding in direction, course, action, opinions." He went on to produce one of his other famous observations which has become much quoted whenever leadership is discussed:

> "Leaders are people who do the right things; managers are people who do things right."

The difference between leadership and management he summarized as activities of vision and judgement – "effectiveness versus activities of mastering routines – efficiency."

For Bennis a leader is someone who is:

- Capable of creating an inspiring vision

- An excellent communicator

- Aware of what challenges have to be met

- Comfortable with change, confusion and constructive conflict

- Able to balance the short and long-term

- A model for integrity

Bennis also talks of a:

> "New leader....commits people to action,......converts followers into leaders, and ....may convert leaders into agents of change."

He outlines four competencies that determine the success of a new leader:

1. The new leader understands and practices the power of appreciation

2. The new leader keeps reminding people of what is important

3. The new leader sustain and generates trust

4. The new leader and the led are intimate allies

Provocatively and after so much research, Bennis argues that leadership is not yet a true 'field' of study. He points out that there are nearly 300 definitions of leadership and that to-date we have no universally agreed-upon set of factors. He does however stress the importance of personal values and he is a very strong advocate of leaders who have the capability to inspire others. He also put forward in his classic work *On Becoming a Leader* the idea that most people "are shaped more by negative experiences than by positive ones".

His latest work, which he co-authored with Bob Thomas, is titled *Geeks and Geezers* and compares the attitudes of leaders under the age of 35 (geeks) with those over age of 70 (geezers) and tries to tease out factors that unite and separate the two groups. One very common factor to emerge with both sets of leaders is the 'crucible' test – a unique life testing experience from which they drew enormous strength. For the geezers it was often the trauma of war. For the geeks brought up in post-war prosperity the crucibles seem to be less dramatic. Nonetheless Bennis and Thomas are able to distil a number of core traits that combine both groups:

1. Adaptive capacity – an ability to survive and adapt to adverse circumstances

2. The ability to create a shared vision. This emphasizes some of Bennis's early work

3. Personal voice – a trait that is centred around strong principles about how people should behave – it might be called character

4. Integrity – the balance of ambition, competence and a morale compass

Essential reading

- *On Becoming a Leader*, Addison-Wesley, Reading MA, 1989

- *Leaders: The Strategies for Taking Charge*, Warren Bennis and Burt Nanus, Harper & Row, 1985

- *The Future of Leadership: Today's Top Leadership Thinkers Speak to Tomorrow's Leaders,* Warren Bennis (Editor) Jossey-Bass

- *Geeks and Geezers,* Warren Bennis and Robert J Thomas, Harvard Business School Press, 2004

Robert Blake and Jane Mouton – The grid people

For some forty years, Dr Robert Blake explored human dynamics via the use of numbers and graphs. Together with his associate Dr Jane Mouton, they developed a company called Scientific Methods Inc in 1961 – it now trades as Grid International. Blake and Mouton were psychologists who went onto develop one of the most significant models in the study of leadership.

Blake received his B.A. degree in psychology from Berea College in 1940 and his M.A. degree in psychology from the University of Virginia a year later. His Ph.D. in psychology was awarded by the University of Texas at Austin in 1947. He continued as a professor at Texas University until 1964.

During his career he also received an Honorary LL.D. in 1992 and lectured at Harvard, Oxford, and Cambridge universities. He spent some of his early years at the famous Tavistock Clinic in London, as a Fulbright Scholar. Dr. Blake was also a Fellow of the American Psychological Association.

Blake and Mouton went on to develop a worldwide network of consultants, co-authored over 40 books and hundreds of articles, and consulted for governments, industries and universities in 40 countries. Their breakthrough text, *The Managerial Grid,* is currently in its fifth edition and has sold over two million copies, and is available in twenty languages. Dr. Mouton died in 1987 whilst Dr. Blake retired in 1998, selling the company to long-time associate Bruce Carlson in 1997. He died in June of 2004.

What are they famous for?

BLAKE AND MOUTON'S MANAGERIAL GRID

Blake and Mouton started from the assumption that a manager's role is to develop attitudes and behaviours in people that promote efficient performance, stimulate creativity and generate innovation. In addition, they believed that it was a manager's role to foster a climate of positive interaction and learning whereby people could develop their capabilities together. Blake and Mouton believed such behaviours could be taught and learned.

The Blake and Mouton Grid was originally developed in 1962 as an organization development model. The framework originated from the idea that there often exists, in the minds of managers, an unnecessary distinction between a concern for people and the accomplishment of tasks. The model put forward the idea that this distinction between people and task is complementary rather than mutually exclusive. They argued that every manager has a clear style of managing that is based on their degree of concern for achieving results (tasks) and concern for people. At one end of the spectrum is the highly task focused manager who is only interested in getting the work completed regardless of the impact on people. At the other end is the manager who believes that people needs must come before any task demands. Blake and Mouton's model showed that there are in fact many different managerial styles that fall between these two extremes.

In reviewing the model it is important to realize that the term 'concern for' does not relate to any specific targets or results achieved. Rather it highlights an individual's general approach and concern for production or task and people demands. For example, a concern for production might not only mean physical products or outputs – it could equally mean the number of new product ideas or the volume of sales or the quality of service offered. A concern for people might include many factors such as friendship, keeping commitments, treating people fairly and acting with integrity.

The Blake and Mouton Grid is a graphic representation of all these different management styles and their identifying characteristics. Once a manager accurately places their own managerial style on the grid, they can then begin to examine its implications. This allows us to then identify any personal or organizational changes that might be needed to improve our performance and the overall working atmosphere.

The grid itself is represented as a chart with two nine-point scales as shown.

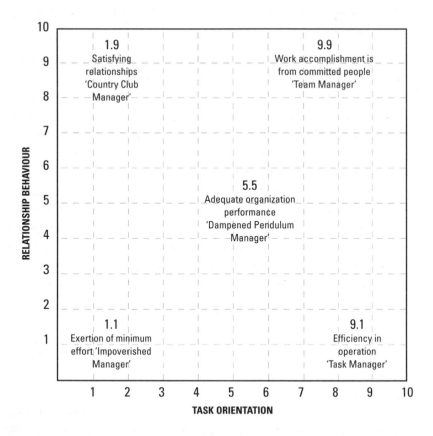

Blake/Mouton Managerial Grid

Whilst the grid indicated a very wide range of possible styles there were five generic types that soon became synonymous with the model and the characteristics they represent still endure in today's corporate world.

THE 9.1 TASK MASTER MANAGER

This style is described as the very pushy and demanding leader – perhaps characterized as the autocrat. For this leader results have to be met at all costs. Any mistakes and errors will be attributed to individuals and blame allocated. This leader always retains control and people are simply expected to comply with any given instructions or commands. Conflict or disagreements with the leader are not tolerated. Any creative talent or energy this manager will have will probably be devoted to political manoeuvrings around the organization or system. The ability to "point the finger" and allocate blame is a key aspect of this leadership style. Blake and Mouton argued that such an approach often results in a highly negative and adversarial employer and employee relationship. The approach might achieve results but it will probably only succeed in the short to medium term.

THE 1.9 COUNTRY CLUB MANAGER

This leadership or management emphasizes a total concern for people. Strongly supportive and encouraging of others, this manager allows people lots of scope and freedom to operate. The team must feel good about themselves and work happily at all times. Rules get in the way of relationships and so informality tends to dominate the working atmosphere. Conflict is frequently avoided and difficult decisions are put off for fear of disrupting team unity and the feelings of goodwill that so often prevail under this style. The end result is often a non-competitive environment and eventually an unsuccessful team that fails to deliver.

THE 1.1 IMPOVERISHED MANAGER

The opting out or non-manager – This is a leader or manager who avoids all decisions and responsibility. They generally allow decisions and events to happen by default. Little or no direction is given to staff or team members and they apply little energy to motivating others. The result that this manager is often described as either 'passed over' or 'failed!' In the medium-term the end result is more often than not a total failure. Managers who end up here are unlikely to survive and would be better suited to apply their energies in another role – perhaps working as some kind of specialist.

THE 5.5 DAMPENED PENDULUM MANAGER

This style can be best described as the middle of the road manager; someone who alternates between the two task and people dimensions and tries to steer a middle course. This leader pushes enough to achieve results but not at the expense of damaging people or morale. For this manager the aim is to achieve an acceptable and working compromise. They apply traditional reward and punishment strategies and seek to avoid 'either or' situations. They will frequently 'split the difference' to achieve a satisfactory solution. To some extent the approach is sub-optimal as it always seeks an acceptable compromise.

THE 9.9 TEAM MANAGER

This style describes the manager who effectively integrates people around the task demands. They always seek the optimal solution and motivate people through a sense of challenge in achieving goals and tasks. This manager liberates and empowers others through a desire for accomplishment. People are encouraged to own their work and solutions thereby generating high levels of commitment and morale. At the same time this manager stresses standards but also encourages healthy conflict in order to achieve the best possible solutions.

In conclusion there is little doubt that Blake and Mouton's Grid has stood the test of time. Even today managers are frequently described as a bit of 'Country Club' type or conversely a hard 'Task Master'. Their model and concepts still resonate today with anyone who has the challenge of managing others or who is on the receiving end of a management style. One of the classic contributions to understanding leadership style.

Essential reading

- *The Managerial Grid*, Gulf Publishing Company, 1964

- *Corporate Excellence through Grid Organization Development*, Gulf Publishing Company, 1968

- *Building a Dynamic Organization through Grid Organization*, Addison-Wesley, 1969

- *Breakthrough in Organizational Development*, Harvard Business Review, 1964 volume 42 no 6 pages 133-55

- *Change by Design*, Addison-Wesley, 1989.

Ken Blanchard – The one minute manager

Dr Ken Blanchard is a prominent author, speaker and business consultant. He is often described as one of the most insightful, powerful and compassionate gurus in the business world.

Blanchard is chairman of Blanchard Training and Development Inc., a management consulting and training company which he founded in 1979. He has regularly appeared on popular television news and business programmes in the US and has been featured in leading magazines such as *Time* and *US News*.

He earned his B.A. in government and philosophy from Cornell University, his M.A. in sociology and counseling from Colgate University and his Ph.D. in educational administration and leadership from Cornell University.

He co-authored the *One Minute Manager Library*, which includes *The One Minute Manager* (1982), *Pulling the One Minute Manager to Work* (1984), *The One Minute Manager Meets the Monkey* (1989), and *The One Minute Manager Builds High Performing Teams* (1990). They've collectively sold more than nine million copies and have been translated into more than 20 languages.

Dr. Blanchard's other books include, *Raving Fans, Everyone's a Coach*, co-authored with Don Shula, former coach of the Miami Dolphins, *The Three Keys to Empowerment: Release the Power within People for Astonishing Results*, co-authored with John Carlos and Alan Randolph. He co-authored *The Power of Ethical Management* and his latest book is entitled *Big Bucks and High Five! The Magic of Working Together.*

What is he famous for?

Blanchard's books are unashamedly simple and clear in both style and content. Forget heavy and turgid academic texts that are rich in references. Blanchard's work often propounds simple messages that seem to register with the millions of people and managers who buy his books. For some he may be overly simplistic and his work might be said to fall into the classic American management literary cliché of 'seven quick steps to happiness and greatness!' But you cannot argue with his success and his populist approach has attracted a strong following around the world.

His classic *One Minute Manager* book which he co-authored with Spencer Johnson (who subsequently went on to write the equally famous and successful *Who Moved My Cheese?* book on change management) epitomized his approach. It became a run away best-seller in the 1980s and spent over two years on the *New York Times* bestseller list; selling over seven million copies around the world. It has also been published in over twenty-six languages.

The book is essentially a clear and simple exploration of what a manager needs to do to be effective. Contained in just 100 pages the book is written in a manner that is accessible, not only to the businessman but also to parents in developing and bringing up children? Full of simple tips and sound people management advice, it is a book that can be read on the move.

Blanchard's leadership approach promotes self-esteem and self worth through a clear and structured approach to making people accountable for their behaviour. The book's central theme – *People who feel good about themselves produce good results* – and appeal is based on applying techniques that take only one minute to apply. Focusing on three fundamental activities the book outlines an approach to:

- **One minute goal setting.** Goals are seen as central to driving success and achievements but they have to be agreed. Once agreed they can be reviewed rapidly and without dispute. The important thing is to take the time to set goals in the first place.

- **One minute praising.** Effective managers have to give praise and ensure that people are rewarded for effective behaviours and performance. Blanchard stresses the need to catch people doing things right.

- **One minute reprimand.** Managers must apply sanctions and reprimands if they are to be effective. By applying one minute reprimands you 'nip things in the bud' and Blanchard again stresses the importance of critiquing the behaviour and not the person. This approach maintains a person's sense of self-worth and integrity. Blanchard recommends reprimanding the behaviour and then encouraging the person to do better by shaking hands.

Essential reading

- *The One Minute Manager,* Ken Blanchard Ph.D and Spencer Johnson MD, Berkley Books New York, 1982

David Brent – aka Rickie Gervais – A modern leadership icon

David Brent was a Regional Manager working in paper distributor Wernham Hogg based in Slough, UK. He first came to wider public notice in the BBC documentary/comedy drama, *The Office* and quickly assumed cult status amongst observers of modern business life. Brent portrayed a very distinctive leadership style that has since provoked much debate and humour throughout organizations and businesses.

Famous for his efforts to integrate his colleagues into an effective team David Brent produced many memorable pieces of philosophy on the art of leading and managing others. He has been described as a philosopher to rival Descartes and portrayed a character that many ordinary people identified from their own 'sad' bosses and work environment. Part monster and lonely, tragic figure, Brent has become a symbol of failed leadership. As much as he has tried to absorb some of the thinking of our other gurus, his defective personality invariably means he interprets it all through a distorted lens. Unfortunately, David Brent is one of those leaders who doesn't know what he doesn't know. His lack of self awareness means he becomes a caricature of the worst type of leader. In his efforts to ingratiate himself to all his team he invariably loses respect and we are left with an uneasy feeling – are we to laugh with him or at him? But his over-sized sense of importance and ego provides a wonderful contrast and counter-balance to some of our conventional gurus.

Here is just a sample of his thoughts on the trials and tribulations of managing and leading people.

On giving a motivational pep talk to his team:

> *"You're all looking at me, your going 'well yeah, you're a success, you've achieved you're goals, you're reaping the rewards, sure. But, OI, Brent is all you care about chasing the Yankee dollar?' Let me show you something I always keep with me. Just a little book,* **Collective Mediations***, and it's a collection of philosophers,*

writers, thinkers, native American wisdom, which I, and it's really showing you that, er, the spiritual side needs as much care and attention as the physical side. It's about feeding the soul, yeah? Evolving spirituality. And a foreword by Duncan Goodhew..."

"Some people are intimidated when talking to large numbers of people in an entertaining way. Not me!"

"If your boss is getting you down, look at him through the prongs of a fork and imagine him in jail."

"If you treat people with love and respect they will never guess that you're trying to get them sacked."

"If at first you don't succeed, remove all evidence you ever tried."

"You have to be 100% behind someone, before you can stab them in the back."

"There may be no 'I' in team, but there is a 'Me' if you look hard enough."

"Know your limitations and be content with them. Too much ambition results in promotion to a job you can't do."

Remember the three golden rules:

1. It was like that when I got here

2. I didn't do it

3. (To your Boss) I like your style

"Avoid employing unlucky people – throw half of the pile of CVs in the bin without reading them."

"Quitters never win, winners never quit. But those who never win and never quit are idiots."

"Process and procedure are the last hiding place of people without the wit and wisdom to do their job properly."

"Put the key of despair into the lock of apathy. Turn the knob of mediocrity, slowly open the gates of despondency – welcome to a day in the average office."

"It's the team that matters. Where would The Beatles be without Ringo? If John got Yoko to play drums the history of music would be completely different."

"When confronted by a difficult problem, you can solve it more easily by reducing it to this question, "How would the Lone Ranger handle this?"

"A problem shared is a problem halved, so is your problem really yours or just half of someone else's?"

"They're malleable, and you know that's what I like really, you know. I don't like people who come here: 'Ooh, we did it this way, we did it that way'. I just wanna do it this way. If you like. If you don't ….. Team playing … I call it team individuality, it's new, and it's like a management style. Again guilty, unorthodox, sue me."

"You don't have to be mad to work here but you do have to be on time, well presented, a team player, customer service focused and sober!"

"I thought I could see light at the end of the tunnel, but it was just another bastard, bringing me more work."

"What does a squirrel do in the summer? It buries nuts. Why? Because then in winter-time he's got something to eat and he won't die. So, collecting nuts in the summer is worthwhile work. Every task you do in work think, would a squirrel do that? Think squirrels think nuts."

"Accept some days you are the pigeon and some days you are the statue."

"Remember that age and treachery will always triumph over youth and ability."

Unfortunately David met his match when he was made redundant at the end of the second series of the programme. Since then he has taken on various sales representative jobs and continues to pop into his old office to see how people are 'missing him' and getting along. Nonetheless, his style and philosophy has left an enduring mark on the leadership map. He is a shining example to all who get leadership seriously wrong. Clearly, his alter ego and creator Ricky Gervais captured a unique perspective on some of the more ridiculous consequences of leadership thinking in today's world. Perhaps David Brent is a real lesson in perspective to us all?

Essential viewing

- *The Office*, Series 1 and 2, BBC Television DVD

Peter Drucker – Management by objectives

Peter Drucker was born in Austria in 1909 and is probably the most renowned business and management guru in the world today. The Harvard Business Review described him as "Father of modern management, social commentator and pre-eminent business philosopher".

Drucker originally trained as a lawyer and then became a journalist on the Franfurter General Anzeiger until the advent of the Nazis. He then moved to London and worked for a group of newspapers, and then as an economics consultant for a number of banks and other financial institutions during the mid 1930s. In 1937 he moved to the United States and started to work in consultancy. By 1943 he was asked to study the policies and structures of General Motors and soon became a key adviser to the organization. In 1945 he published *The Concept of the Corporation* and became the first real management thinker or guru.

During his career he has held three key positions; professor of philosophy and politics at Bennington College, then Professor of Management at New York University. From 1971 he has been Clarke Professor of social science and management at Claremont Graduate School in California.

A prolific author he has written over 20 books that have sold millions and been translated into dozens of languages around the world. He also has lectured in oriental art and written two novels.

He has advised many of the world's major businesses and has constantly aimed to keep ahead of trends by actually developing them rather than following them.

What is he famous for?

"There is no substitute for leadership. But management cannot create leaders. It can only create the conditions under which potential leadership qualities become effective; or it can stifle potential leadership."

Whilst Warren Bennis has been termed the Dean of leadership gurus, it is Peter Drucker who has been most associated with actually inventing the business guru world. Recognized as a true original thinker his work, *The Practice of Management*, published in 1954 was a blueprint for introducing the world to professional management. English academic and political scientist Cyril Northcote Parkinson, once described Drucker as practically inventing management philosophy after discovering that the Americans were interested in business but that no such philosophy existed. Although he has argued that leadership is innate and that as a result it cannot be taught or promoted, he contributed massively to the development of the manager's role in the organization.

It was in his work *The Concept of the Corporation* that Drucker first mentioned his famous concept of 'management by objectives' (MBO). This was a management term that became synonymous with Drucker. He argued that all managers should be driven by objectives.

"Objectives are needed in every area where performance and results directly and vitally affect the survival and prosperity of the business."

Management by objectives became the critical process through which individual performance and in turn business performance would be delivered.

But it was *The Practice of Management* that really brought him to the attention of the wider business world. Whilst it covered a wide range of topics and was very strong on defining the role of a business as being to simply create customers, the book's major contribution was in defining the essence of the manager's role in the newly developing corporate world. One of Drucker's core propositions is that management impacts on all aspects of life and has become a defining influence to everyone on the planet.

For him managers are central to organizing work and making effective decisions in order to achieve successful business performance. Interestingly, Drucker chose not to make profit maximization the ultimate goal for a business. For him profit maximization is neither the cause of business behaviour nor the rationale for business decision-making. Rather profit is the test of the success or robustness of any business model or enterprise. The central question for Drucker is how best to organize a business so that profits can be made and the enterprise can endure and succeed over time? His philosophy that the purpose of any business is to create customers comes through in much of his writing. Indeed, some of these concepts seem exceedingly attractive in today's obsessively short-term and excessively financially driven world where customer service is frequently sacrificed in the face of saving another euro or dollar in costs.

Drucker saw the need for clear objectives as central to the business model he was advocating and he listed eight critical business areas that required set targets:

- Market standing
- Innovation

- Productivity

- Physical and financial resources

- Profitability

- Manager performance and development

- Worker performance and attitude

- Public responsibility

The above list is all the more remarkable when you reflect that he was writing it some fifty years ago. Measures, Drucker constantly argued, are important because they make things visible and real. It is measures, he argues, that help managers to focus and decide upon priorities. He also stressed the importance of management as a resource and encouraged the continued development of it. To him management was the vital resource needed to sustain and grow organizations.

People needed to avoid what he termed the three forces of misdirection in the modern corporation. These forces were:

1. The increasing specialization of managerial work

2. Hierarchy

3. The differences in business direction that can exist in a business

If these forces were not correctly managed then there was an increased likelihood of conflicts and clashes occurring within an organization. So Drucker advocated Management by Objectives (MBO) as a means by which managers could overcome these potentially negative forces by linking their individual work to a set of wider organizational goals. Of course this linking of individual and corporate performance is a major challenge that even today exists in most businesses. MBO was a process that provided feedback and enabled individuals to grow in their roles and develop their capabilities – to be able to identify both their strengths and development needs. For Drucker the MBO process enabled a manager to become more effective for the benefit of the organization.

Drucker also argued that MBO increased the motivation of managers and developed their commitment to the organization. The result was that common people could collectively achieve uncommon performance in terms of wider organizational goals. Yet when MBO was actually implemented in organizations the reality was that many leaders failed to recognize some of Drucker's deeper insights into human motivation. The result was that MBO soon became a rather crude, simplistic and, in many corporations, bureaucratic targeting mechanism. By the late 1970s it was seen as a rather out-dated and old fashioned concept. Although it is probably true to say that all of today's corporate performance management systems are un-deniably based on the fundamentals of Drucker's MBO system.

In addition to focusing on the role of the manager Drucker has always been concerned with the larger landscape of business and organizational thinking. As far back as 1974 in his book *Management* he commented:

> *"The most important change for management is that the aspirations and values and the very survival of society in the developed countries will come to depend on the performance, the competence, the earnestness and the values of its managers."*

Given some of the observations made elsewhere in this book about the current leadership agenda the fact that Drucker was talking about the central importance of values some 30 years ago is all the more remarkable. Whilst advocating the importance of people in business he has also always argued that it is the rational and logical side of the brain that should govern a leader or manager's actions. This of course places him at odds with current gurus like Goleman and Kouzes and Posner who advocate an understanding of the more emotional side of leadership as a guiding compass for leadership action.

Drucker has also been critical of the behaviour of recent CEO's who have earned enormous sums whilst laying off thousands of staff – "You have no idea how contemptuous this makes midlevel managers". He cites the example of reading a book about Marco Polo in which he asked Genghis Khan what he expected of his officers. And he said, "Of an officer I expect that he takes care of the men before he takes care of himself. Of a general I expect that he takes care of his horse before he takes care of his men". When Polo asks why? He said "An officer leads by doing and a general leads by example". Drucker argues that today's CEOs violate that principle with exorbitant compensation for eliminating employees. He has described it as a "terrible trend".

In recent years Drucker has switched his attention to the emerging trends of the 21st century, the global economy, the rise of the knowledge worker and new forms of organization. In doing so he has arguably created words such as *knowledge worker* and *privatization*.

In his 1996 work *Leaders of the Future* he described leadership as:

> *"The core characteristics of effective leaders... include basic intelligence, clear and strong values, high levels of personal energy, the ability and desire to grow constantly, vision, infectious curiosity, a good memory and the ability to make followers feel good about themselves... Built on [these] foundation characteristics are enabling behaviours... including empathy, predictability, persuasive capability, the ability and willingness to lead by personal example and communication skills... It is the weaving together, the dynamic interaction, of the characteristics on a day-by-day, minute-by-minute basis that allow truly effective leadership."*

Drucker is a true giant in all fields of leadership and management thinking.

Essential reading

- *Managing in Turbulent Times*, Harper Business, 1980
- *The Practice of Management*, Harper Business, 1954
- *Managing for Results*, Heinemann, London, 1964
- *The Effective Executive*, Harper Business, 1967

Fred Fiedler – The contingency theory man

Fred Edward Fiedler was born in Vienna, Austria on 13 July, 1922. Fiedler is a globally recognized name in the academic field of psychology and leadership. He has authored or co-authored more than 200 scientific papers and several books. His articles are frequently cited by others and have been published by the most respected journals in the fields of psychology, leadership and management.

After completing secondary school, he served a brief apprenticeship in his father's textile business before emigrating to the United States in 1938. Fiedler developed an interest in psychology in his early teens from reading his father's books on the topic. He served in the US Army from 1942 to 1945 and took several extension courses in psychology while serving. In 1946 he re-entered the University of Chicago to study psychology – his study had been interrupted by Army service. He subsequently received a master's degree in industrial and organizational psychology in 1947 and his Ph.D. in clinical psychology in 1949.

While at the University of Chicago he was a trainee and then a research assistant with the Veterans Administration (VA), and continued working for a year after his graduation as a research associate and instructor for the VA in Chicago. Following a summer in the Combat Crew Research Laboratory at Randolph Field, he became associate director on a naval research contract at the University of Illinois' College of Education. His work during this period with Donald Fiske and Lee Cronbach sparked his lifelong interest in leadership.

From 1950 until 1969, Fiedler was on the faculty of the University of Illinois, where he initiated and directed the Group Effectiveness Research Laboratory (GERL). In 1969 Fiedler moved to the University of Washington where he remained on the faculty until his retirement in 1993. There he established the Organizational Research Group and directed the Group Effectiveness Research Laboratory. His wife became assistant director of the University of Washington's Educational Assessment Centre.

Fiedler has held research fellowships at the University of Amsterdam from 1957 to 1958, at the University of Louvain in Belgium from 1963 to 1964, and at Templeton College, Oxford from 1986 to 1987. He has also served as a consultant for various federal and local government agencies and private industries in the United States and around the world.

Fiedler was recognized by the American Psychological Association for counselling research in 1971 and for his contributions to military psychology in 1979. He received the Stogdill Award for Distinguished Contributions to Leadership in 1978. The American Academy of Management honoured Fiedler as a Distinguished Educator in Management in 1993, and the Society for Industrial and Organizational Psychology recognized his outstanding scientific contributions in 1996. In 1999 the American Psychological Society presented Fiedler with its James McKeen Cattell Award.

What is he famous for?

In the late 1940s the emphasis in leadership research shifted from traits and the personal characteristics of leaders to leadership styles and behaviours. From the late 1960s through the 1980s, leadership interests again shifted to the concept of contingency models of leadership. One of the earliest and best known is Fiedler's contingency model of leadership effectiveness. Published in 1967 as *A Theory of Leadership Effectiveness*, the model immediately drew attention as the first leadership theory to measure the interaction between leadership personality and the leader's situational control in predicting leadership performance.

While many scholars assumed that there was one best style of leadership, Fiedler's contingency model argues that a leader's effectiveness is based on 'situational contingency', or a match between the leader's style and situational favourableness, later called situational control. More than 400 studies have since investigated this relationship and many other gurus in this book pick up on this theme.

A key component in Fiedler's contingency theory is the least preferred co-worker (LPC) scale, an instrument for measuring an individual's leadership orientation using eighteen to twenty-five pairs of adjectives. Respondents are asked to consider the person they liked working with the least, either presently or in the past, and to rate them on each pair of adjectives. High-LPC or relationship-motivated leaders describe their least preferred co-worker in positive terms and are concerned with maintaining a good interpersonal relationship. Low-LPC or task-motivated leaders describe their least preferred co-worker in negative terms, and give a higher priority to the task requirements than to the personal relationship.

According to Fiedler, there is no ideal leader. Both low-LPC (task-oriented) and high-LPC (relationship-oriented) leaders can be effective if their leadership orientation fits the situation. Three components determine what Fiedler termed the level of situational favourableness or control:

1. Leader-member relationships: the degree to which the employees accept the leader.

2. Task structure: the degree and level of detail to which subordinate roles and jobs are defined.

3. Position power: the amount of formal authority a leader possesses by virtue of their position in the organization.

Fiedler found that low-LPC leaders are more effective in extremely favourable or unfavourable situations, whereas high-LPC leaders perform best in situations with intermediate favourability.

Since personality is relatively stable, the contingency model suggests that improving effectiveness requires changing a situation to fit a particular leader. The organization or the leader can decide to increase or decrease the level of task structure and positional power, whereas training and group development activities may lead to improved leader–member relations.

Fiedler's contingency theory has drawn criticism because it also implies that in some situations the only alternative for a mismatch between a leader's orientation and an unfavourable situation is changing the leader. Despite this, Fiedler and his associates have provided decades of research to support and refine the contingency theory. Cognitive resource theory (CRT) modifies Fiedler's basic contingency model by adding traits of the leader to the concept. Cognitive resource theory tries to identify the conditions under which leaders and group members will use their intellectual powers, skills and knowledge effectively. While it has been generally assumed that more intelligent and more experienced leaders will perform better than those with less intelligence and experience, this assumption is not supported by Fiedler's research.

To Fiedler, stress is a key determinant of a leader's effectiveness and a distinction is made between stress induced by a leader's boss or superior, and the stress induced by subordinates or the situation itself. In stressful situations, leaders dwell on the difficult relationships with others and find it more difficult to focus their intellectual abilities on the job. Thus, intelligence tends to be more effective and used more frequently in stress-free situations. Fiedler has found that experience tends to impair performance in low-stress conditions but contributes greatly to performance under high-stress conditions.

In conclusion Fiedler's work and theory advocated that:

1. The favourableness of leadership situations should be assessed in determining leadership effectiveness.

2. Candidates for leadership positions should be evaluated using the LPC scale.

3. If a leader is being identified for a particular position, then a leader with an appropriate LPC profile should be chosen (task-orientated for very favourable or very unfavourable situations and relationship-orientated for intermediate favourableness).

4. If a leadership situation is being chosen for a particular candidate, a situation (work team, department, etc.) should be

chosen which matches their LPC profile (very favourable or unfavourable for task-orientated leaders and intermediate favourableness for relationship-orientated leader).

Now in retirement, Fiedler continues to inspire and encourage research on leadership and other related topics. Fiedler and his contingency theory of leadership rightly achieved a prominent place in the history of management thought. He was one of the first to recognize and produce a leadership model that combines personality traits and contextual factors. The more recent cognitive resource theory promises to extend his influence many years into the future.

Essential reading

- *A Theory of Leadership Effectiveness*, New York, McGraw-Hill, 1967

- *Leadership*, New York, General Learning Press, 1971

- *Leader Attitudes and Group Effectiveness*, Westport, CT, Greenwood Publishing Group, 1981

- *Leadership Experience and Leadership Performance*, Alexandria, VA, US Army Research Institute for the Behavioural and Social Sciences, 1994

- *Leadership and Effective Management*, Fiedler, F.E. and Chemers, M.M. Glenview, IL, Scott, Foresman and Co., 1974

- *New Approaches to Leadership, Cognitive Resources and Organizational Performance*, Fiedler, F.E. and Garcia, J.E. New York, John Wiley and Sons, 1987

Daniel Goleman – The emotional intelligence (EQ) man

Professor Daniel Goleman was born in Stockton California and studied at Amherst College and then Harvard where he obtained a PhD in clinical psychology. Subsequently he studied at Yale and then went onto Rutgers University Graduate School of Applied and Professional Psychology in Piscataway, New Jersey. At Rutgers he runs the Consortium for Research on Emotional Intelligence in Organizations. He was also science correspondent for *The New York Times*.

Dr. Goleman has received many journalistic awards for his writing, including two nominations for the Pulitzer Prize for his articles in *The Times*, and a Career Achievement Award for Journalism from the American Psychological Association. In recognition of his efforts to communicate the behavioural sciences to the public, he was elected a Fellow of the American Association for the Advancement of Science.

What is he famous for?

In the last few years Daniel Goleman has had a huge impact on the leadership debate through his concept of Emotional Intelligence (EQ). In fact, his name has now become synonymous with the concept of EQ and he can be said to have invented a whole new field involving the study of leadership. His ground-breaking book written in 1995 has since sold in excess of five million copies and initiated a whole new leadership development and consulting field. The book was on *The New York Times* bestseller list for a year-and-a-half, and has been a bestseller throughout Europe, Asia and Latin America. It has also been translated into nearly 30 languages. His ideas have also been adopted by the education sector and are being applied in schools to help children develop emotional intelligence.

His central argument is that for too long the business world has stressed the importance of 'thinking' intelligence at the expense of what he has termed 'emotional intelligence.' He argues that we should measure emotional intelligence as much as traditional thinking intelligence (IQ) in order to really understand leadership effectiveness.

For Goleman it is essential that a leader be able to read social and political currents in an organization.

> "Every organization has its own invisible nervous system of connection and influence... Some people are oblivious to this below the radar world, while others have it fully on their own screen. Skill at reading the currents that influence the real decision-makers depends on the ability to empathize on an organizational level, not just an interpersonal one."

Central to his work is the belief that the most important act for a leader is in creating and driving positive emotions in others. He also argues that it is possible for people to develop their emotional intelligence – unlike IQ – but he also insists that in order to succeed in developing emotional intelligence people have to understand in the first place how they learn. They then need to be able to re-programme or re-wire how their brain responds to given situations.

His work cites five components of emotional intelligence (EQ) as illustrated in the following table opposite.

	DEFINITION	HALLMARK
SELF AWARENESS	The ability to recognize and understand your moods, emotions and drives, as well as their effect on others	Self confidence Realistic self-assessment Self deprecating sense of humour
SELF REGULATION	The ability to control or redirect disruptive moods or impulses To think before acting – to suspend judgement	Integrity and trustworthiness Comfort with ambiguity Openness to change
MOTIVATION	A passion to work for reasons beyond pay or status A propensity to pursue goals with energy and determination	Strong desire to achieve Optimistic even in the face of failure
EMPATHY	Ability to understand the emotional makeup of people Skill in treating people according to their emotional reactions	Expertise in building and retaining talent Cross cultural sensitivities Service to customers
SOCIAL SKILLS	Good in managing relationships and building networks Able to find common ground and rapport	Effectiveness in leading change Persuasiveness Expertise in building and leading teams

Goldman believes that our emotions frequently conflict with our thinking intelligence, such that our own logical response to a situation is frequently contradicted by our emotional response. In measuring the prescribed aspects of EQ he believes that we can achieve a better understanding of ourselves and how we relate to other people.

Goldman developed his concept to specifically look at leadership and to examine how EQ might influence a leadership style. He developed six possible approaches:

1. Visionary Leadership

2. Coaching Leadership

3. Affiliative Leadership

5. Democratic Leadership

6. Pace Setting Leadership

7. Commanding Leadership

For Goldman it is the moods and behaviours of leaders rather than their knowledge or vision that has most impact on how people work. He argues that many leaders lack self-awareness and as a result remain blocked in understanding their real impact on others' lives. For a leader this inability to assess their impact on others is a major disability.

He has also written *The New Leaders*, which explores in greater depth the application of his theories to leadership. The message is that emotionally intelligent leaders are now 'must haves' for business and the book details some practical guidelines to implement the concepts.

In 2003 he also published *Destructive Emotions*, an account of a scientific dialogue between the Dalai Lama and a group of psychologists, neuroscientists and philosophers.

Essential reading

- *Emotional Intelligence*, Bloomsbury Publishing, 1996

- *Working with Emotional Intelligence*, Bloomsbury Publishing, 1999

- *The New Leaders – Transforming the Art of Leadership into the Science of Results*, Bloomsbury Publishing, 2002

Paul Hersey – Situational leadership

Dr. Paul Hersey is a behavioural scientist whose ideas have been used to train managers around the globe for more than thirty years. Founder and CEO of the Centre for Leadership Studies, he has helped train more than four million managers from over 1,000 organizations worldwide, including Mobil, IBM, Caterpillar, Harris and Illinois Bell. In the middle 1960s, Hersey's research at the Centre for Leadership Studies led to the development of the Situational Leadership Model, an approach to leadership that has become widely accepted in the United States and other countries.

Hersey joined Ohio University as Professor and Chair of the Management Department in 1966, and left in 1975 to develop his leadership centre. He has been recognized for his contributions to leadership studies by the Academy of Management and the American Society for Training and Development.

He first published his major ideas in articles in the early 1960s and in 1969 he wrote a textbook containing the Model, *Management of Organizational Behaviour*. This classic text has been translated into 14 languages and has sold more than a million copies worldwide.

With experience of presenting his Situational Leadership Model and ideas in more than 125 countries, Hersey continues to provide training and consulting expertise in leadership, management, education, sales, program development and research. He was also awarded the

1997 Award for Achievements in Business by the College of Business at Ohio University.

What is he famous for?

Paul Hersey produced a classic management model that has had a huge impact on leadership practices. Called Situational Leadership it is a highly practical framework that bases effective leadership around the situation rather than any need for specific personality traits. Hersey argues that his model is organized common sense and he points out that its enormous success is based on the fact that it is a model rather than a theory. He argues that the model addresses behaviours rather than attitudes or personal values and as behaviours are more flexible and easier to adapt than values people can apply the model without fear of changing their personality or values. Like John Adair, Hersey focuses on individual effectiveness – what you do – rather than who you are and your personality.

Hersey's model has been used in thousands of organizations around the world and remains a powerful model in helping managers and leaders on a day to day basis. It is one of the few models that brings immediate and practical insights to a leader's day to day work. In many ways it builds on the works of Fiedler and Blake and Mouton but takes the approach to a far more practical and applied manner.

Hersey worked originally with Ken Blanchard (of *The One Minute Manager* fame) to produce the Situational Leadership Matrix. But it appears they subsequently decided to go their different ways with the result that Blanchard now promotes a similar model but with a different language and terminology. The main contribution of the model to leadership thinking was in further breaking the myth that there exists one ideal leadership style. Following the thinking of Fiedler and others, Hersey argues that effective leaders adapt their style to suit different situations. He then went on to develop a model that helps people obtain the right balance between delegating tasks and controlling or directing the work of others. His model proposes four generic leadership styles in which he differentiates between directive and supporting strategies:

FOUR LEADERSHIP STYLES

1. **Telling**. Highly directive and for individuals who are new to their work and need to be supervised closely

2. **Selling**. Very directive and supportive for individuals who need to have their confidence developed

3. **Participating**. For individuals who need some support to build their confidence and motivation or to deal with difficult issues

4. **Delegating**. For competent and committed individuals who do not require too much direction or support

TWO LEADERSHIP STRATEGIES

1. **Directive**. Giving individuals clear instructions and direction about how, when and where to do things

2. **Supportive**. Listening and encouraging the involvement of others in problem-solving

Hersey's model is based on the classic premise that there are two major dimensions that help to shape a leadership style:

- The amount of emphasis placed on a task being executed correctly and precisely. The more a manager stresses the task then the more directive their behaviour is likely to be. In other words, the manager specifies:

  1. What they want done

  2. How they want it done

  3. When they want it done

- The amount of emphasis placed on the relationship support given to people when being managed. The more this factor is stressed then the more likely the leader will actively encourage and praise good work and seek to develop strong and supportive working relationships.

The relationship between these two factors can be shown in the form of Hersey's matrix comprising the four distinctive leadership styles.

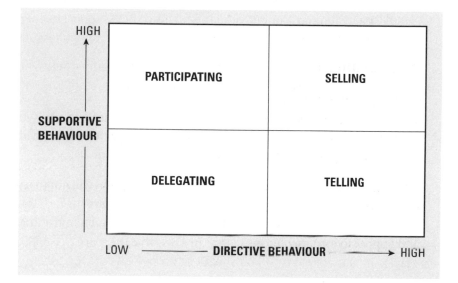

Telling Style

HIGH TASK – LOW RELATIONSHIP

The leader who uses this style closely controls the work of their staff and acts quickly to correct and re-direct any falls in performance. They make sure people are clear about what tasks they have to accomplish and emphasize the use of standard procedures – stressing at all times the importance of targets and deadlines.

Selling Style

HIGH TASK – HIGH RELATIONSHIP

The leader who uses this style shows a concern for the task as well as staff relationships. They may spend time in friendly or supportive conversation, but they also make sure people are clear about their individual responsibilities and the standards of performance required. They may sometimes incorporate staff ideas into any decisions, but ultimately the leader retains overall control of the task and how it is completed.

Participating Style

LOW TASK – HIGH RELATIONSHIP

The leader who uses this style allows people to manage their own work. They do not lead or direct staff in any strong direction or manner. Rather the leader allows individuals to set their own goals.

Such leaders are available for discussion and advice, but will not push their own ideas. They rely on the self-guidance and direction of the individual but also make people feel valued – offering encouraging and supportive contributions.

Delegating Style

LOW TASK – LOW RELATIONSHIP

The leader who uses this style effectively liberates or empowers people to define problems and develop solutions by themselves. They do not intervene but make themselves available if required by adopting a distant but supportive position.

Hersey argues that the effective leader switches between the different styles according to the 'maturity or readiness level' of people to complete any given task. For the model maturity or readiness involves two elements.

MOTIVATION

Is the individual motivated and willing to do the task/work?

COMPETENCE

Is the individual competent to do the work? Have they the necessary skills, knowledge and experience to complete the task?

By combining the dimension of employee readiness with the notion of task and relationship management Hersey's model produces a highly effective approach to help managers find the best leadership style to any given situation.

Telling Style

Where individuals have low competence and low motivation or lack confidence, an effective manager will provide close supervision or direction. For example, with new staff it is essential that close attention is paid to clarifying their role and responsibilities. Attempts to use participating or selling styles may be less effective because, whilst good relationships may be established, people need to have clarity of their tasks and to know exactly what is expected of them.

It is important to remember that this style is not in any way aggressive or overbearing. Rather it is the mark of a leader who is simply being clear and precise in what is required. If people don't know how to do something and lack confidence, then the best way to get the job done is to tell them how to do it.

Selling Style

As an individual's maturity gradually increases, so the effective leader tries to encourage this by becoming more supportive. If they were to continue to be strongly directive, staff might start to become resentful and demoralized. So a good leader wants to begin to growth the confidence of people. At this stage they cannot jump to a participating style because people are not yet considered 'mature' or competent enough to make the right decisions without the leader's input. So the leader must still provide clear direction on how a job or task should be completed.

This is perhaps the style that most managers will adopt with enthusiastic people who have just joined the organization.

Participating Style

As people mature they become more competent and motivated in their roles. An effective leader will no longer need to emphasize how a task or job should be completed. They can in effect start to step back on the understanding that the individual knows what they are doing. Consequently the participating style concentrates on establishing close productive relationships.

Delegating Style

When an individual possesses a very high level of maturity – they are both able and motivated – an effective leader can step back thereby providing additional motivation by delegating responsibility to the individual. It is important to note that this phase does not involve abdication as the leader is still available to discuss any matters that arise. But the leaders will only really intervene at the request of the staff or team member.

Hersey argues that when a performance problem occurs, an effective leader can move back to a previous and more directive style if required. Equally, if performance is good a leader can move forward a stage and reduce the amount of task control they provide. Hersey stresses the need for consistency and warns that too many changes in style can result in confusion and uncertainty. The worst leaders are those who continually jump from one end of the scale to another, such as moving from a delegating to telling style. In such circumstances managers may complain about the unwillingness of staff to assume responsibility whilst their people will complain about being confused and de-motivated by this sudden and radically different communications style.

Developing any leadership style is a challenging task and perhaps few people get it right all the time. Situational Leadership however, provides a simple and elegant way of matching individuals and situations with appropriate leadership direction. It is a wonderfully practical and helpful contribution to the study of leadership. Little wonder that millions of managers have been trained in the model and techniques.

Essential reading

- *The Situational Leader*, New York, Warner, 1984

Manfred Kets de Vries – The psychology of leadership

Manfred Kets de Vries is another member of the small group of non-American gurus to feature in our list of influential figures. He holds the Raoul de Vitry d'Avaucourt Chair of Human Resource Management, and is Clinical Professor of Management and Leadership at INSEAD.

He has also held professorships at McGill University, the École Hautes Études Commerciales, Montreal, and the Harvard Business School.

In 1977 he undertook psychoanalytical training at the Canadian Psycho-analytical Institute and in 1982 became a member of the Canadian Psychoanalytical Society and the International Psychoanalytical Association. As well as working as a psychoanalyst he combines his clinical background with the study of leadership.

He did a doctoral examination in economics at the University of Amsterdam and holds an ITP certificate from Harvard. In addition, he has a master's degree and a doctoral degree in business administration from Harvard Business School.

He is author of over 100 scientific papers and several leadership books, and combines a busy academic career with working as a psychoanalyst and consulting to some of the world's major corporations.

The Dutch Government has also made him an Officer in the Order of Oranje Nassau. He was the first fly fisherman in Outer Mongolia and is a member of New York's Explorers Club. In his spare time he can be found in the rainforests or savannas of Central Africa, the Siberian Taiga, the Pamir Mountains, or the barren wastelands of the Arctic.

What is he famous for?

Kets de Vries work provides unique perspectives and insights into the personality traits associated with leadership. Unlike many other gurus he probes deeper into the human psyche and explores the 'darker side' of leadership, along with notions of the narcissistic personality and charisma. His work might be described as putting "leadership on the couch" as he seeks to explore leadership from the non-rational as opposed to rational side that dominates so much of leadership thinking in the corporate world.

"My aim in demonstrating the use of the clinical paradigm has been to open the eyes of organizational participants, to make them realize what can and cannot be done, to recognize their strengths and weaknesses and to prevent executives from getting stuck in vicious circles, and to make them understand the cause of resistance to change. My intention has been to widen their choice. Is that not what mental health is all about?"

His work offers many fascinating glimpses in the flawed nature of leadership and the addictiveness of power. At the same time his work explores the impact of leadership in developing high performance organizations and effective working environments.

His leadership work has led him to explore in depth the leadership styles of many current and recent leadership icons including Richard Branson (Virgin), Percy Barnevik (formerly of ABB) Jack Welch (formerly GE), Walt Disney and Ernest Saunders (formerly of Guinness).

"Branson, Welch and Barnevik all have something of the showman in them."

He is quoted as saying that many leaders are hooked on the four 'Ps' namely Power, (the) Podium, Perks and Praise. In citing some reasons for leadership incompetence he cites:

1. The unwillingness to exercise authority – which may result in either the avoidance of conflict situations or the constant need to be liked

2. The tyranny of subordinates as caused by an excessively abrasive set of behaviours

3. Micro-management and the obsession with detail

4. Overly political game playing.

On a more positive note he also draws analogies of effective leadership with the running of small jazz bands and advocates the coaching, mentoring and cheerleader side of leadership that promotes:

- The relentless pursuit of a vision combined with a dissatisfaction with the traditional approach and method

- Strategic awareness throughout an organization

- Genuine leadership behaviours – walking the talk and setting a clear example

- A genuine appreciation of people and interpersonal skills

- A strong value on cross-cultural and emotional skills

- An ongoing commitment to education.

For the jazz combo read a working environment where people are able to work together but at the same time express individuality and improvise. His work is probably most fascinating when probing the darker side of leadership but he has also contributed practical advice and guidance on developing leadership. His checklist of excellent leadership practices includes the following:

- Provide vision

- Are strong communicators

- Create high levels of trust

- Acquire emotional intelligence (EQ)

- Motivate and stretch people

- Build teams

- Provide constructive feedback

- Modify their narcissistic needs to the benefit of the organization

- Are persistent and decisive

- Are good time managers

- Possess a sense of humour

He also coined the wonderful phrase 'The Teddy Bear Syndrome' when talking of certain charismatic leaders who have a very rare ability to make other individuals feel that they are the most important people in the world to them. Such comments have been made of Nelson Mandela and former US President Bill Clinton; the effect they can have on a first meeting being to overwhelm people with their sense of genuine interest and respect. Like the child's teddy bear you appear to be the most important person in the world to them.

Kets de Vries work provides us with unique insights into the leadership psyche and provides a very rich and interesting contrast to the work of other leadership gurus.

Essential reading

- *The Neurotic Organization: Diagnosis and Changing Counter-Productive Styles of Management*, Jossey Bass (1984, 1990 with D. Miller)

- *Leaders, Fools and Impostors*, Jossey Bass, 1993

- *Life and Death in the Executive Fast Lane: Essays on Organizations and Leadership*, Jossey Bass, 1995

- *The Leadership Mystique: A User's Manual for the Human Enterprise*, Financial Times, Prentice Hall

John Kotter – The leader and change

Harvard Business School professor John P Kotter runs a close second to Warren Bennis' mantel as the world's foremost leadership guru.

Born in California in 1947 he originally trained as an electrical engineer at Massachusetts Institute of Technology before moving into the world of management. In 1972 he gained his PhD at Harvard and became a full professor – one of the youngest in the university's history – in 1980 from where he has continued to work.

Kotter is the author of *The Heart of Change* (2002), *John P. Kotter on What Leaders Really Do* (1999), *Matsushita Leadership* (1997), *Leading Change* (1996), *The New Rules* (1995), *Corporate Culture and Performance* (1992), *A Force for Change* (1990), *The Leadership Factor* (1988),

Power and Influence (1985), *The General Managers* (1982), and five other books published in the 1970s. His books have been reprinted in 80 foreign language editions and total sales are approaching two million copies. His articles in the Harvard Business Review have sold a million and a half copies.

Kotter's awards include an Exxon Award for Innovation in Graduate Business School Curriculum Design and a Johnson, Smith and Knisely Award for New Perspectives in Business Leadership. In 1996, *Leading Change* was named the top management book of the year by *Management General* and in 1998, *Matsushita Leadership* won *The Financial Times/Booz·Allen and Hamilton* Global Business Book Award for biography/autobiography. In October 2001, Business Week magazine rated Kotter the number one 'leadership guru' in America based on a survey they conducted of 504 enterprises.

What is he famous for?

"Most organizations are over-managed and under led."

In 1996 John Kotter wrote his bestselling book *Leading Change* which detailed a highly successful mandate for leading organizational change. The work set him aside as one of the most influential and important writers on leadership in current times. His theory that "managers promote stability, leaders press for change and only organizations that embrace both sides of that contradiction can survive turbulent times" was put forward in his work *A Force for Change*.

For Kotter some people can make great managers but not leaders and vice versa. Whilst management is about coping with complexity, leadership is about coping with change. Leaders, he argues, involve others and seek to enhance self-esteem. In *Leading for Change* Kotter identified eight critical stages that leaders need to follow in order to achieve effective organizational transformation. He detailed the stages as follows:

ESTABLISH A SENSE OF URGENCY

A key to the successful leadership of change is the need to create a sense of real urgency – "If you don't start with a sense of urgency, the change programme will eventually collapse". Kotter argues that over half the companies he observed in his research were never able to create enough urgency to drive real action and change. "Without motivation, people won't help and the effort goes nowhere.... Executives underestimate how hard it can be to drive people out of their comfort zones". In successful change, leaders facilitate an open discussion on tough or difficult issues. In addressing the question 'when is the urgency level high enough for change to occur? Kotter suggests it is sufficient when 75% of the leadership group is convinced that business as usual is no longer an acceptable strategy.

FORM A POWERFUL GUIDING COALITION

Change efforts often start with just one or two people and should grow continually to include more supporters for the change. Developing a ground swell of support is critical to success. Any initial group needs to be politically powerful in order to harness resources and get things done. The building of this coalition and developing the sense of urgency about what is needed is crucial to success.

CREATE A VISION

Successful transformation rests on "a picture of the future that is relatively easy to communicate and appeals to customers, stockholders and employees. A vision helps clarify the direction in which an organization needs to move". The vision functions in many different ways: it helps promote motivation and helps keep the changes on track. It will also act as a compass bearing in difficult times.

COMMUNICATE THAT VISION

Kotter suggests the leadership should estimate how much communication of the vision is needed, and then multiply that effort by a factor of ten. Kotter argues, "A useful rule of thumb: if you can't communicate the vision to someone in five minutes or less and get a reaction that signifies both understanding and interest, you are not yet done with this phase of the transformation process". Kotter also says that leaders must be seen 'walking the talk' – another form of communication – if people are going to perceive the effort as important. 'Deeds' along with 'words' are powerful communicators of any new changes. Typically, change efforts fail unless people understand, appreciate, commit and try to make the change happen.

EMPOWER OTHERS TO ACT ON THE VISION

To enable real change to occur, people also need to be freed up from existing responsibilities. Leaders need to remove any obstacles preventing or blocking the change and this may mean empowering others to challenge and break down barriers.

PLAN FOR AND CREATE SHORT-TERM WINS

Real change or transformation takes time and frequently there is a threat of set backs and a loss of momentum. This needs to be avoided. In successful change, leaders actively plan and deliver some form of short-term gains to enable people to see progress and celebrate success. Kotter points out, "When it becomes clear to people that major change will take a long time, urgency levels can drop. Commitments to produce short-term wins help keep the urgency level up and force detailed analytical thinking that can clarify or revise visions".

CONSOLIDATE IMPROVEMENTS AND KEEP THE MOMENTUM FOR CHANGE MOVING

Kotter warns, "Do not declare victory too soon". Leaders of successful efforts use the benefits of success as the motivation to drive more change deeper into the organization. They seek to go on and identify more ways in which people, processes and systems can be changed.

They do not expect instant gains but instead see the journey of change as a long one that may take several years.

INSTITUTIONALIZE THE NEW APPROACHES

Change only ever takes root when it becomes 'the way we do things around here'. This requires real behavioural change – "Until new behaviours are rooted in social norms and shared values, they are subject to degradations as soon as the pressure for change is removed". To offset this threat Kotter argues that any new approaches need to be institutionalized and quickly supported by all parts of the organization. It is only when people start to genuinely live the change that it will become a reality.

The Kotter framework towards transformational change is used by some of the world's top companies and it has even been adopted by the US military.

One of Kotter's other big contributions has been, like Warren Bennis, to compare management with leadership. His analysis derived four key distinctions:

1. The Agenda – he argues that managers tend to be interested with planning and budgeting within specific timeframes. In contrast, leaders work to create a vision and tend to operate on broader horizons and so bring other people in and align them towards the vision. Interestingly Kotter argues that vision is not a mystical or nebulous concept, rather he describes it as providing a simple but powerful focus.

2. Managers focus on how best to structure the organization or draw the organization chart whilst leaders stress the importance of communications. Aligning people around a vision is a communications rather than design challenge for any leader. This is one of the big assets of any true leader.

3. Managers focus on problem-solving while leaders aim to inspire and motivate the organization to higher performance. Management controls people by pushing them in the right

direction; leadership motivates people by satisfying basic needs. Leadership aims to satisfy people by providing achievement, belonging, recognition, self-esteem and self-control – this in turn provokes a deep seated motivational response that can lead to extraordinary results and accomplishments.

4. Managers tend to focus on results and this leads them to naturally stress continuity and predictability in business processes and models. In effect, they manage complexity. In contrast Kotter argues that leaders see their job as constantly creating and managing change.

Kotter is clear that whilst these differences exist it is nonetheless possible for one individual to carry out both roles. However, what is important is that the individual knows that the specific tasks are indeed very different. Whilst management majors on the present, leadership is all about focusing on the future. This analysis led him to make his famous observation on organizations being "over managed." The dilemmas posed by this observation are illustrated in the model below:

Management Skills

CREATING AN AGENDA: PLANNING AND BUDGETING

- Setting targets/goals

- Establishing detailed steps

- Allocating resources

BUILDING A NETWORK TO ACHIEVE THE AGENDA: ORGANIZING AND STAFFING

- Creating an organizational structure and set of jobs

- Staffing with qualified people

- Communicating the plan

- Delegating responsibility for carrying out the plan

- Devising systems to monitor and control

EXECUTION: CONTROLLING AND PROBLEM SOLVING

- Monitoring performance to plan

- Identifying significant deviations

- Planning and organizing to solve problems

OUTCOME: PRODUCING STABILITY

- Produces predictability and order

- Ensures expected results

Leadership skills

CREATING AN AGENDA: SETTING DIRECTION

- Developing a vision for the future

- Developing strategies for producing the changes needed to achieve the vision

BUILDING A NETWORK TO ACHIEVE THE AGENDA: ALIGNING PEOPLE

- Communicating the direction by words and deeds

- To create teams and coalitions committed to working to achieve the vision

EXECUTION: MOTIVATING AND INSPIRING

- Energizing people to overcome obstacles in the way of change

- By appealing to basic needs, values and emotions

- By empowering people to act

Continued over...

OUTCOME: PRODUCING CHANGE

- Produces change

- Ensures adaptation to a changing environment

Source: J Kotter, A Force for Change

Clearly, Kotter agrees with Warren Bennis on the importance of vision and longer-term planning horizons. He also argues that leadership skills can be acquired and developed in others. He disregards the idea that simple entrepreneurial ability is sufficient to make good leaders. Kotter advocates identifying talented people early on in their career and then developing their leadership skills systematically over time.

In 1996 he wrote a book on the life of Konosuke Matsushita who built a business empire worth some $80 billion including the mighty Panasonic brand. In commenting on Matsushita and comparing him with Nelson Mandela, he was once quoted as saying:

"Typical of all great leaders, they had enormous personal strength and conviction, and they had a driving passion to make their leadership vision a social and organizational reality."

Kotter's views on leadership appear accurate and insightful as we enter the millennium with other more traditional approaches struggling with the ongoing tide of down-sizing, de-layering and off-shoring. For Kotter the future is about the emergence of a new leadership 'substance' which does not depend upon power but rather upon networking and influence.

In one of his most recent works, *The Heart of Change*, which he wrote along with Dan Cohen, he researched over 100 organizations in the middle of major change programmes. Their observations led them to conclude that managers were mistaken in trying to change people's thinking. What they should be trying to do, they argue, is change people's feelings. Kotter argues, "When it comes to behavioural change, it is much less about using data to change the way people think and how they behave, than it is about, say, something that is surprising or dramatic or emotionally compelling". This is what he labels the difference between 'see-feel- change' and 'analysis-think-change'. Kotter's assertion is the former moves people more to action. In the new world Kotter argues that, "Leadership is about actualizing potential and then using those skills and abilities".

Essential reading

- *Leading Change*, Harvard Business School Press, 1996

- *The New Rules: How to Succeed in Today's Post-Corporate World*, Free Press, 1995

- *A Force for Change: How Leadership Differs from Management*, Free Press, 1988

- *What Leaders Really Do*, Harvard Business School Press, 1999

- Article: *Leading Change: Why Transformation Efforts Fail*, Harvard Business Review, March-April, 1995

- *The Heart of Change*, Harvard Business School Press, 2002

James M Kouzes and Barry Posner – Leadership and followership

Jim Kouzes and Barry Posner are major researchers, award-winning writers and consultants in the field of leadership and executive development.

Jim Kouzes is Chairman Emeritus of the Tom Peters Company. He is also an executive fellow at the Centre for Innovation and Entrepreneurship at the Leavey School of Business, Santa Clara University.

Barry Posner received his undergraduate degree in political science from UC Santa Barbara and his master's degree in public administration from Ohio State University. His Ph.D. is in organizational behaviour and administrative theory from the University of Massachusetts, Amherst.

Posner is currently Dean of The Leavey School of Business and Professor of Leadership at Santa Clara University (Silicon Valley, California), where he has received numerous teaching and innovation awards. He is a renowned scholar who has published more than 80 research and practitioner-oriented articles in journals such as *The Academy of Management Journal, Journal of Applied Psychology, Human Relations* and *Personnel Psychology*. He is currently on the editorial review boards of the *Journal of Business Ethics* and *Leadership Review*, and section editor for the *Journal of Management Inquiry*.

Kouzes and Posner were named by the International Management Council as the 2001 recipients of the prestigious Wilbur M. McFeely Award. This award places them in the company of Ken Blanchard, Stephen Covey, Peter Drucker, Edward Deming, Lee Iacocca, Rosabeth Moss Kanter and Tom Peters, all of whom were earlier recipients of the award.

Both are frequent conference speakers and have conducted leadership development programmes for hundreds of organizations.

What are they famous for?

"Leadership is in the eye of the follower."

Kouzes and Posners' studies, pioneered in 1983, led them to create a model of leadership that has been embraced by more than one million people around the world. They could be said to belong to the new school of transformational leadership thinking; whereby a leader is viewed as having the ability to fundamentally transform an organization through a powerful perspective and a distinctive set of capabilities. Central to their work is the belief that it is followers who make leaders powerful: Napoleon without an army was just a man with grandiose ideas.

This model was presented in their award-winning and best-selling leadership book *The Leadership Challenge: How to Keep Getting Extraordinary Things Done in Organizations*. Described as a ground-breaking piece of research study, *The Leadership Challenge* combines keen insights with practical applications. With over one million copies in print, this book has been the featured selection of several book clubs, named book-of-the-year by the American Council of Health Care Executives and received the Critic's Choice Award from the American book review editors. It has since been translated into over 15 foreign languages.

In their study, Jim Kouzes and Barry Posner set out to discover what it took to become a great leader. They wanted to know the common practices of ordinary men and women when they were at their best in leadership roles. Based on some 20 years of research of cases and surveys (they developed a huge database about leadership) and from this they have distilled five simple principles of leadership which they term:

THE FIVE PRACTICES OF EXEMPLARY LEADERSHIP

1. **Model the Way.** Leaders establish principles concerning the way people (constituents, peers, colleagues and customers) should be treated and the way goals should be pursued. They create standards of excellence and then set an example for others to follow. Because the prospect of complex change can overwhelm people and inhibit action, they set short-term goals so that people can achieve small wins as they work toward larger objectives. They unravel bureaucracy when it prevents action being taken. Such leaders also clearly provide direction for people at times of uncertainty and create opportunities for victory.

2. **Inspire a Shared Vision**. Leaders passionately believe that they can make a difference. They see a vision of the future and in doing so create a compelling image of what the organization can become. Through their magnetism and quiet persuasion, leaders enlist others in their visions and dreams.

They breathe life into their visions and motivate people to see exciting possibilities in the future.

3. **Challenge the Process.** Leaders constantly search for opportunities to change the status quo. They look for innovative ways to improve the organization. In doing so, they experiment and take risks. Because they know that risk taking involves mistakes and failures, they accept the inevitable disappointments that might result.

4. **Enable Others to Act.** Leaders cultivate strong and mutual collaborations with others. They build spirited teams and actively involve others. Leaders understand that mutual respect is what sustains extraordinary efforts; they strive to create an atmosphere of trust and human dignity. They strengthen others, making each person feel capable and powerful.

5. **Encourage the Heart.** Accomplishing extraordinary things in organizations is hard work. To keep hope and determination alive, leaders recognize the contributions that other people make. In every winning team the members need to share in the rewards of their efforts, so leaders celebrate accomplishments. They make people feel like heroes and apply lots of energy to building the right atmosphere.

An immediate reaction to some of Kouzes and Posners work is that it smacks of 'American Apple Pie.' It sounds delicious but at the same time it can seem very idealistic. Many people are perhaps put off by the strong emotional language they use in describing their ideas and concepts. There is no doubt that it is too "touchy feely" for some more cynical managers. But perhaps that is what their work is challenging us to think about – leadership is about stretching our thinking and extending our views of what is possible beyond the rational and scientific approach to business. For them leadership is all about creating an emotional connection with people. If we accept that emotional commitment is a more powerful driver of individual behaviour than intellectual understanding then they no doubt have a strong case.

Certainly their work puts them on the newer emotional side of leadership study.

Essential reading

- *The Leadership Challenge: How to Keep Getting Extraordinary Things Done in Organizations*, Jossey Bass Wiley, 2003

- *Encouraging the Heart: A Leader's Guide to Rewarding and Recognizing Others*, Jossey Bass, 1998

Nicolo Machiavelli – The Prince

Nicolo Machiavelli (1469-1527) was perhaps the first great political philosopher of the Renaissance period. His famous treatise, *The Prince*, written in 1513 and published after his death in 1532, stands apart from all other political writings of the period in that it probed the very practical problems a monarch faced in trying to stay in power.

As a result of this work, Machiavelli has become an enduring symbol of the world of realpolitik – governmental policy based on retaining power rather than pursuing ideals.

Nicolo Machiavelli was born in Florence, Italy at a time when the country was in political disarray. Italy was divided between four dominant city-states and each of these was subject to intense foreign interference.

In 1434, Florence was ruled by the powerful Medici family but in 1494 their rule was temporarily halted by a reform movement, led by Piero Soderini, in which Machiavelli became an important figure and diplomat. The Medici family regained power in 1512 with the aid of Spanish troops. By this time Machiavelli had been removed from public life and was in fact subjected to torture. For the next 10 years he devoted himself to writing history, political philosophy and plays. Amazingly

Machiavelli regained favour with the Medici family and was called back to public duty for the last two years of his life.

Interestingly, his works were not published in English for another century.

What is he famous for?

Machiavelli's great contribution to leadership was to become the first person to highlight and explore the darker side of leadership, and notions of expediency and ruthless power. He described a world of political cunning, intrigue and brutality. More interesting is that even after over 500 years his legacy lives on in today's world. His work is very much an exploration of power; how to achieve it and how to hold on to it. Still today, any form of manipulative organizational or political behaviour is frequently described as being Machiavellian.

There is no question that Machiavelli's thinking still reverberates in the minds of many and he might be said to be simply representing the reality of political life, both inside and outside organizations. In effect, Machiavelli gave credence to the belief that for a leader it was acceptable to do whatever it takes. He was the first champion of opportunism over morality.

The Prince, when first published, immediately provoked controversy and was condemned by Pope Clement VIII. Many viewed his work as a treatise on the acceptance of tyranny as a viable means of leadership. The book's main theme is that princes should retain absolute control of their territories, and they should use any means of expediency to accomplish this end, including deceit. He argued that a leader "should know how to enter into evil when necessity commands".

Academics have sometimes struggled over interpreting Machiavelli's precise intent in writing the work. Machiavelli praises Caesar Borgia, a Spanish aristocrat who became a notorious and ruthless tyrant of the Romagna region of northern Italy. During Machiavelli's years as a diplomat, he witnessed Borgia's rule and some commentators have argued whether or not Machiavelli was holding up Borgia as the role model prince?

Other readers initially saw *The Prince* as a satire on absolute rulers such as Borgia, which showed the horror of arbitrary and unbridled power. However, this theory collapsed when, in 1810, a letter written by Machiavelli was discovered. In the letter he reveals that he wrote *The Prince* to ingratiate himself towards the ruling Medici family and, in particular, the Prince Guiliano de Medici.

Machiavelli begins *The Prince* by describing the two principal types of governments: monarchies and republics. He then centres on monarchies and describes the real truths about surviving as a monarch. Rather than recommending high moral ideals he delves into the darker recesses of the human psyche. In doing so he lists certain virtues that a successful prince needs to possess if they are to succeed. However, he also concludes that some of these 'virtues' will lead to a prince's destruction, whereas other 'vices' will allow the prince to survive. But in typical fashion he wrote:

"It is unnecessary for a prince to have all the virtues, but necessary to appear to have them."

Indeed, the very virtues that we might commonly praise in people, Machiavelli argues, might lead to a prince's downfall. For example, we might commonly believe that it would be best for a prince to enjoy a reputation for generosity. However, he argues that if this generosity is given in secret, then no one will know about it and consequently a prince may be thought of as being selfish and greedy. If, on the other hand, the prince is very open and generous he might ultimately lose his wealth with the result that he might then be forced to extort more money from his subjects and thus become a hated figure. For this reason Machiavelli concluded that it was perhaps best for a prince to cultivate and enjoy a reputation for being rather mean.

Recognising and accepting that human nature is fickle meant that the effective prince knew how to instil fear in his subjects so that they would not betray him. Machiavelli argued that it is better for a prince to be severe rather than merciful when punishing people for crimes. Demonstrating severity through awarding death sentences may affect only a few but he argued that it would help to deter crimes that ultimately impact on many people. Ruthlessness in Machiavelli's terms meant the inability to demonstrate pity or compassion to others. In dealing with enemies he argued that the prince needed to be fast and decisive.

One of his most famous quotes on leadership is:

> "It is best for a leader to be loved but if they cannot be loved they must be feared"

A prince, he argued, could easily avoid hatred by not confiscating the property of his subjects:

> "People more quickly forget the death of their father than the loss of their inheritance."

Perhaps the most controversial section of *The Prince*, is where Machiavelli explores the really dark side of leadership and argues that the prince should know how to be deceitful when it suits his purpose. When the prince needs to be deceitful, though, he must not appear that way. Indeed, he must always exhibit five virtues in particular: mercy, honesty, humaneness, uprightness and religiousness. It is this application of two faced, double dealing behaviour that Machiavelli has become synonymous with. It is all about the ability to tell a story that you do not believe in with real credibility. Integrity and ethical behaviour, it seems, had little to do with his world.

> "A prince ought to have no other aim or thought, nor select anything else for his study, than war and its rules and discipline; for this is the sole art that belongs to him."

His advocates would say that in writing the work, Machiavelli has simply set out an honest assessment of life and the political world. His detractors argue that it is a deeply cynical view of life. Certainly, Machiavelli exposes the darker side of leadership; a side that stands in marked contrast to many of the works of today's human centred leadership studies. Yet in a very real sense his work seems more relevant today than ever, especially when discussing the nature of leadership. The recent corporate scandals in the United States and Europe have provided very vivid examples and confirmations that unbridled and absolute power has the ability to corrupt on a massive and destructive scale. Those managers who operate in any large organization will know that Machiavelli's strategies and tactics are clearly followed by some colleagues. In summary, a classic work on leadership.

Essential reading

- *The Prince*, Oxford University Press Publishing (Peter Bond-anella Translator) Paperback – February 2005

Abraham Maslow – The motivation man

American psychologist, Dr. Abraham Maslow was one of the original founders of human psychology and played a key role in helping leaders understand the concept of motivation.

Born in New York in 1908, Maslow's PhD in psychology was awarded in 1934 at the University of Wisconsin and formed the basis of all his motivational research. He later moved to New York's Brooklyn College. He died in 1970.

The following quote perhaps best sums up his approach to understanding people.

"Many things in life cannot be transmitted well by words, concepts, or books. Colours that we see cannot be described to a man born blind. Only a swimmer knows how swimming feels; the non-swimmer can get only the faintest idea of it with all the words and books in the world. The psychopath will never know happiness or love. The youngster must wait until he is a parent in order to know parenthood fully and to say 'I didn't realize.' My toothache feels different than your toothache. And so it goes. Perhaps it is better to say that all of life must be first known experientially. There is no substitute for experience, none at all."

What is he famous for?

Abraham Maslow's key message was that certain needs are a fundamental part of human nature. Values, beliefs and customs might differ from country to country and group to group, but all people he argued have similar needs. Leaders, he stressed, needed to understand the importance of these needs because of their inherent motivational power.

In 1943 he published *A Theory of Human Motivation* in the *Psychological Review Journal* and set out his memorable 'Hierarchy of Needs Theory'. In it he argued that basic human needs were arranged in a hierarchical order. His theory was based on the study of healthy, creative people who were able to use all their talents, potential and capabilities. At the time of publication Maslow's research approach proved a very important distinction to most other psychological research of the period. The vast majority of research in the field tended to be based on observations of the mentally ill, so Maslow was quite unique in focusing on the mentally well and healthy. His first key book, *Motivation and Personality*, was subsequently published in 1954.

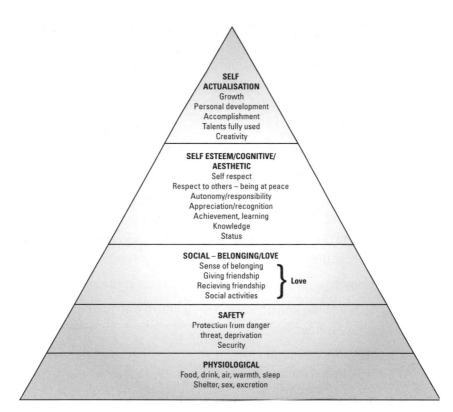

Abraham Maslow defined individual needs in this pyramid

Maslow's model asserted that a higher human need, what he termed self-actualization, is only expressed after certain lower level motivational needs are met or fulfilled. His work was hugely influential for the leadership and organization world as it generated a whole new debate around individual motivation and the need to satisfy his fundamental needs.

Maslow defined two major groups of human needs which he termed basic and meta needs.

Basic needs are physiological (such as food, water and sleep) and psychological (such as affection, security and self esteem).These can also be described as deficiency needs because if they are not met, the individual will seek to make up any deficiency.

Maslow described the higher meta needs as growth needs. These include justice, goodness, beauty, order and unity, etc. He argued that human nature is such that basic needs take priority over growth needs. People who lack food or water cannot attend to concepts such justice or beauty. But once these are met people will tend to move on to the growth needs.

The needs are listed below in a hierarchical order.

7. **Self-actualization**- A state of well-being, knowing exactly who you are, where you are going and what you want to accomplish in life.

6. **Aesthetic** – being at peace, more curious about the inner workings of things.

5. **Cognitive** – learning for learning alone, contribute knowledge.

4. **Esteem** – feeling of moving up in the world, recognition, few doubts about self.

3. **Belongingness and love** – belonging to a group, having close friends to confine with.

2. **Safety** – feeling free from immediate danger.

1. **Physiological** – food, water, shelter, sex.

Maslow argued that people are forever striving to satisfy these various needs and that because lower level needs are more immediate and urgent, if they are not satisfied then they come into play as the primary motivational goal for driving individuals. Higher needs in the hierarchy only come into play so long as lower needs have been satisfied. Lower needs that remain unsatisfied will prevail and must be satisfied before individuals can climb up the hierarchy of remaining needs.

To summarize, the needs on the bottom of the list (1 to 4) have to be met before any of the above needs can be addressed. The top four needs (5 to 7) can be pursued in any order so long as all the other needs (1 to 4) have all been met.

Knowing where someone is located on this scale provides a simple way of determining motivation strategies. For example, motivating a secure professional worker (who is in range 4 of the hierarchy) with a certificate for achievement will have a far greater impact than using the same motivation tool on someone earning a very poor wage and living in tough circumstances struggling to meet even their basic needs.

No one stays in a part of the hierarchy for an extended period of time. Maslow argued that we constantly strive to move up, while at the same time forces, often outside our control, attempt to push us down. Even those people at the top of the hierarchy eventually get pushed down for some time, e.g. the death of a loved-one or a work project that fails. Conversely, those people on the bottom of the scale get pushed up, e.g. they win the lottery or receive a better paid job.

The goal of leaders, Maslow argued, was to help people obtain the skills and knowledge that push them up the hierarchy permanently. Behind this work was one of the central assumptions of the human relations school of management, of which Maslow was a key founder. Happy people are productive people. They are able to concentrate on fulfilling positive futures instead of consistently having to worrying about how to make ends meet.

In describing someone who attains the highest level of need satisfaction – self actualization – Maslow detailed the following characteristics:

MASLOW'S CHARACTERISTICS OF SELF-ACTUALIZATION

- Possesses a clear sense of reality – is aware of real situations and applies objective rather than subjective judgements to the situation

- Views problems in terms of challenges that require solutions

- Has a need for privacy and is comfortable being alone

- Relies on their own experiences and judgement – is independent – does not necessarily rely on any external culture or environmental factors to form opinions and views

- Not susceptible to social pressures – non-conformist

- Is democratic and fair – embraces and enjoys all cultures, races and individual styles

- Socially compassionate – humane

- Accepts others as they are – does not try to change people

- Comfortable with oneself – despite any unconventional tendencies

- Possesses a few close friends rather than enjoying many superficial relationships

- Can laugh at self – has a sense of humour directed at oneself or the human condition, rather than at others

- Is spontaneous and natural – true to oneself, rather than trying to meet others needs

- Excited and interested in everything

- Creative, inventive and original

- Seeks out peak experiences that leave a lasting impression

The work of Abraham Maslow occupies a central position in popular psychology and is the foundation upon which humanistic management models were first developed. His work helped leaders to understand human behaviour and for that reason he needs to be included in our list of gurus.

Essential reading

- *Motivation and Personality*, Harper and Row, New York, 1954

- *Toward a Psychology of Being*, Abraham H. Maslow, Richard J. Lowry (Editor) John Wiley & Sons Inc

- *Maslow on Management*, John Wiley & Sons Inc, 1998

- *Motivation and Personality*, Robert Frager (Editor), Longman Paperback, 1987

Douglas McGregor – The theory X and theory Y man (or carrot and stick approach)

Douglas McGregor was born in 1906 and he stayed in academia for most of his working life. He studied first at Antioch College but from 1954 until his death in 1964 he worked at the Massachusetts Institute of Technology, where he was Professor of Management.

Whilst favouring the academic world his career was characterized by a desire to bridge the gulf between the behavioural sciences and management practices. He was a central figure in the Human Relations School that started to develop in the late 1950s and 1960s. His work is generally quoted alongside Abraham Maslow's motivational research.

What is he famous for?

"The motivation, the potential for development, the capacity for assuming responsibility... are all present in people. Management does not put them there."

McGregor's greatest contribution was a simple theory of motivation that he outlined in his seminal work *The Human Side of Enterprise*. His theory has had a huge impact on the way people think about leading, managing and designing successful organizations. His theory became universally known as Theory X and Theory Y.

Douglas McGregor believed that the primary role of a manager was to manage other people in accomplishing tasks and objectives. The starting point for any leader was to examine how they saw their role and relationships to other people. However this examination needed to be based on a perception, of not just the world in which the leader functioned but also how they viewed the people operating in that world. McGregor then set out two fundamental beliefs or assumptions about individual motivation and based it on two theoretical constructs concerning the nature of people and their relationship to work:

Theory X assumptions include the following:

1. People are inherently lazy and will avoid work if they can.

2. People, because they dislike work, must be driven, directed, coerced, controlled, or threatened with punishment in order to get them to work as their organization requires.

3. The average human being prefers to be directed, wishes to avoid responsibility, has relatively little ambition and wants security above all else.

Theory Y assumptions about human motivation included the following:

1. The expenditure of physical and mental effort in work is as natural as play or rest. The ordinary person does not dislike work: according to conditions it may be a source of satisfaction or punishment.

2. External control and the threat of punishment are not the only means of motivating people to work toward organizational goals. Individuals will exercise self-direction and self-control towards objectives that they are committed to.

3. The most significant reward that can be offered in order to obtain commitment is the satisfaction of the individual's needs. (Self Actualization was the term used by Abraham Maslow to describe this level of higher order motivational needs.)

4. The average human being learns, under proper conditions, not only to accept but also to seek responsibility.

5. The capacity for exercising a relatively high degree of imagination, ingenuity and creativity in solving organizational problems is widely, not narrowly, distributed in the population.

6. At present the potential of the average person is not being fully used.

Clearly, Theory Y assumptions reflect an essentially optimistic view of human nature. It sees unlimited potential in people for personal and organizational growth. In contrast, Theory X represents a static and pessimistic view of individuals. They have to be driven hard to perform.

The motivating forces contained in the assumptions of Theory Y are those similar to the rewards that are described in Abraham Maslow's *Hierarchy of Needs*. In other words, Theory Y management aims to integrate individual goals with those of the organization – making a job the principal means through which people can enlarge their competence, self-control and sense of accomplishment. In such an atmosphere, Theory Y holds that people are more likely to identify with the goals of an organization because the organization identifies with their goals. Control then becomes internally directed by the individual rather than externally, as is implied by Theory X. In Theory X external control is essential and it generally comes from strong and directive management supervision, accompanied by the imposition of rules and constraints.

McGregor argued that depending on the assumptions that were adopted, a leader would then have a clear rationale for developing the right organization policies, structures and practices. The result was that some people concluded that the role of a leader rested on a choice being made between two extreme positions: You can choose to be either a 'hard' or 'soft' leader.

Hard leadership is characterized by the use of excessive control and in some cases coercion and threats to obtain performance from others. Soft management is characterized by the leader who strives to satisfy individual demands and promotes a harmonious working atmosphere with the result that high levels of performance then follow.

Interestingly, McGregor saw the hard and soft management debate as irrelevant because it ignored or misinterpreted the key findings of his research. For him, leadership direction and control, whether accomplished through the 'hard' or 'soft' approach, was insufficient to motivate people. McGregor argued that real motivational needs are based primarily in the social and egotistic dimensions of people.

According to him, Theory X and Y does not explain human nature, instead it simply illustrates what happens to people and production as a result of a leader's actions.

So what of his contribution to the field of leadership? Well, it is clear that while many companies articulate ideals involving empowerment and growing individuals, many continue to operate an essentially carrot and stick approach to influence behaviour. Essentially, we might argue that the foundation of McGregor's work is the notion of 'trust' and the ability of a leader to invest in it.

Essential reading

- *The Human Side Of Enterprise*, McGraw Hill, 1960
- *Leadership and Motivation*, MIT Press, 1966

David McClelland – Achievement, affiliation and power motivation

David McClelland was born in 1917and became a Boston-based psychologist whose behavioural science work influenced three generations of organizational behaviour specialists. His extensive fields of research covered several areas of business-related and organizational behaviour issues.

An expert on human behaviour, he achieved his doctorate in psychology at Yale in 1941 and became professor at Wesleyan University. McClelland went on to become a distinguished Research Professor of Psychology at Boston University and a Professor Emeritus of Psychology at Harvard University in Cambridge Massachusetts. He also founded and directed in 1983, McBer, a specialist human resources management and consulting firm that was subsequently acquired by the Hay Consulting Group.

A fellow of the American Academy of Sciences and the author of several books including *Personality, The Achievement Motive,* and *The Achieving Society,* McClelland received a Guggenheim Fellowship in 1958.

He died in March, 1998.

What is he famous for?

McClelland is chiefly known for his work on achievement motivation, but his research interests also extended to other aspects of the human personality and consciousness. He pioneered motivational thinking in the workplace and in turn developed a unique motivational theory. He was also arguably at the forefront of developing the whole field of competency analysis together with competency based assessments and tests. Concepts that now dominate many human resource processes and approaches in major organizations. His proposition was that these motives and competencies were better predictors of individual performance than many traditional IQ and personality-based tests. His ideas have since been widely adopted in many organizations across the globe.

David McClelland described three types of fundamental motivational needs, which he identified in his book, *Human Motivation*:

- Achievement Motivation (N-Ach)

- Power Motivation (N-Pw)

- Affiliation Motivation (N-Aff)

These motivational needs or motives are found in varying degrees in all of us and their exact mix helps characterize our own behaviours and, in turn, management style. An understanding of these motives provides leaders with a series of strategies and mechanisms to motivate the different types. By providing the right conditions managers can arouse certain motivations and in turn the desired work behaviours.

NEED FOR ACHIEVEMENT MOTIVATION (N-ACH)

The achievement motivated person is driven by a need to achieve for themselves. This is an important distinction as they are not seeking to achieve in order to impress others, rather they are seeking to compete with themselves and improve their own sense of accomplishment. As a result they seek the attainment of goals and targets to satisfy that motivation. In setting goals, they are adept at assessing risk and they have a strong need for performance feedback in order to allow them to regulate their performance. They will naturally tend to be task focused and possess a need to control situations in order to ensure they can deliver the required results. This drive will also prompt individuals to develop real expertise in order to increase the likelihood of delivering the desired goals or accomplishments. In some cases they may not like to delegate or let go as they fear losing control and not being able to deliver the results they want.

To get the best out of these people McClelland argued that they needed to be allowed to have access to expertise, be allowed to set challenging but realizable goals and have the authority to take control. It is also important that a strong task focused climate is encouraged around any challenges. Achievement motivated people tend not to want to waste time on activities that are not central to the accomplishment of the task. In that sense they can be quite matter of fact and not have time for excessive relationship issues or concerns. It is about getting the result and then resetting the bar for the next target.

NEED FOR POWER MOTIVATION (N-PW)

The power motivated person has a need to be seen as, or viewed as, influential by others. They are people who have a strong desire to impact on others in some way. McClelland identified this motive as the most complex and he detailed four specific types of power motivation:

Stage one power is a desire to belong to something or someone that is perceived as powerful and influential. For some people this could be a job role such as Executive Assistant to the Chief Executive. Alternatively, it could consist of belonging to a group or club that is regarded as influential or positive, such as an elite military unit, police force or top selling sales team or indeed, a local football team. The motivation comes from the sense of belonging to a powerful or influential source such as the Chief Executive. It is this source that generates the sense of motivation.

Stage two power is about feeling in control and maintaining your independence regardless of anyone else. Managers who take full control and do not worry about challenges or threats from others are good examples. In fact, the more they might be challenged then the more independent and assertive they become. 'No one tells me what to do in this office' is the hallmark of a strong stage two manager. Typically they are the bosses who run their operation as they wish and no one can tell them how to do it.

Stage three power motivation is the motive most closely associated with leadership and management. This individual is motivated by the act of directing or influencing other people. In other words, they like the sense that comes with having power to influence and direct others. Interestingly, McClelland differentiated between social and personalized stage three power with the later being perhaps the more Machiavellian and self-interested, whereas socialized stage three power is all about influencing for the greater good. When one thinks of certain political and business leaders one can easily see the difference. Richard Nixon might have been said to be all about personalized power whereas someone like John F Kennedy certainly tried to lead for a greater good. Some of the corporate leaders that we have been critical of in our introductory chapter might be said to have been very stage three motivated – they want to lead people and direct them. However when we look at the detail of how they operate it does tend to show lots of personalized power needs. In other words it is all about them and serving their narrow needs and agendas rather than worrying about the wider needs of staff and shareholders.

Stage four power reflects inter-dependence – a desire not to control or influence people directly but simply to act as a conduit for liberating other people to assume greater things. This is a rather complex notion but it can be best described as akin to the guru style. Take for example, someone like Ghandi. He was able to create a major transformation in India yet he did so wearing sack cloth clothes and working from a basic farm. He simply saw himself as an instrument of a higher force for good. Some people argue this concept is very much what today's managers need to aspire to – they have to become coaches and facilitators, rather than heroic leaders in the classic sense.

People who are power motivated often have a need to gravitate to leadership roles. In some of the stages there is also a need to acquire the trappings associated with personal and organizational status and prestige. The size of office and car are seen as symbols of one's power.

To motivate these people, McClelland argued that they need to be allowed to participate in important endeavours and to have the opportunity to lead and assume positions of authority. Naturally, they also respond to the prizes that accompany such power, or what Manfred Kets de Vries terms the four Ps – Power, Perks, Praise and the Podium.

NEED FOR AFFILIATION MOTIVATION (N-AFF)

The affiliation motivated person has a need to develop close friendly and personal relationships. They are motivated by interactions with other people. The affiliation motive produces a need to be liked and held in popular regard by others. These people are often strong team players and possess high levels of empathy and human understanding. They contribute strongly to building team spirit and possess excellent interpersonal skills.

This motive is more often seen in organizations where there is a sense of public service and a need for empathy, such as health care and other caring professions.

To motivate these people effectively, leaders have to ensure that the culture or climate surrounding them is both healthy and supportive. It is also likely that they respond better to fundamental human needs rather than appeals for financial or commercial gain.

Originally it was thought that achievement motivated people made the best managers and leaders. McClelland detailed the following as characteristics of the achievement motivated manager:

- Achieving the task or goal is more important than any material or financial reward.

- Achieving the task provides far greater satisfaction than receiving recognition. The motivation comes from within and not externally as for the power motivated individual.

- Financial reward is regarded as a measure of success and not an end in itself.

- Neither security or status are primary concerns or motivators.

- Performance feedback that is reliable and factual is critical because it enables performance to be improved over time.

- Achievement motivated people constantly seek improvements and innovative ways of doing things.

- Achievement motivated people prefer roles and responsibilities that satisfy their basic needs. Ideally such roles will offer flexibility and the opportunity to set and achieve challenging goals.

For a long time it was felt that Achievement Motivation was the most desirable attribute in leaders. But, in actual fact, McClelland went on to conclude that it was power motivated individuals that often made the best leaders. Whilst the achievement motivated individual was often the innovative entrepreneur, it was the power motivated leader who had the inherent motivational pattern to build and lead people on a very large scale.

When reviewing these motives it is important to point out that McClelland saw effective performance as a function of three factors, Motivation x Abilities x the Situation. It is not enough that someone is simply power motivated and will therefore make a good manager.

They also need to possess the necessary skills to function successfully in the role.

In conclusion McClelland provides a very useful understanding of human motivation that has not enjoyed the widespread acclaim of some of our other gurus. Yet his work on leadership and power motivation is a very stimulating and interesting addition to the leadership field.

Essential reading

- *Human Motivation*, Cambridge University Press, 1998

- *The Achieving Society*, Van Nostrand, The Free Press, 1961

- Article: *Power is the Great Motivator*, Harvard Business Review

Tom Peters – The revolutionary leadership guru

Tom Peters might be said to have invented the modern day business of management gurus. *The Los Angeles Times* said, "Peters is … the father of the post modern corporation". While *The New Yorker* magazine reported, "In no small part what American corporations have become is what Peters has encouraged them to be".

He trained originally as an engineer, gaining a masters degree in civil engineering at Cornell University. He then served in Vietnam with the US army. Later he took an MBA and PhD at Stanford Business School and then worked at the Washington Office of Management and Budget. He subsequently joined McKinsey consultants in 1974 and left in 1981, after becoming a Partner in their Organization Effectiveness practice in 1979.

He holds many honorary degrees including one from the State University of Moscow.

He is founder of the Tom Peters Group and a prolific writer and speaker whose presentations are legendary for their high octane energy and radical fervour.

What is he famous for?

"So now the chief job of the leader; at all levels, is to oversee the dismantling of dysfunctional old truths, and to prepare people and organizations to deal with them – to love, to develop affection for- change per se, as innovations are proposed, tested, rejected, modified and adopted.

Lead by empowering people. Become a compulsive listener. Cherish the people at the front-line. Delegate effectively. Bash bureaucracy."

Nearly 20 years ago McKinsey consultants Tom Peters and Robert 'Bob' Waterman wrote a book titled In *Search of Excellence.* At the time of writing the US business world was under attack from the enormous rise of Japan as an industrial nation. The US was experiencing 10% unemployment and interest rates of 20%. It seemed as if the US economy and business world was being steam-rolled into the second division of competitiveness. The idea for the book fell out of a small McKinsey project that was not even viewed as main stream to the normal McKinsey focus on strategy.

Peters and Waterman essentially went out to investigate what smart US companies were actually doing at that difficult time. The result was a slow burning bestseller that effectively invented the new world of quality, customer quality and what every other organization has since been doing to gain a competitive world class edge. The book arguably started the revolution in the US and European business world and catapulted Peters to the status of a major global business guru. The book cited 43 excellent companies and included names such as IBM, Hewlett Packard and 3M. It is now generally regarded as a business classic.

The book highlighted a model called the 7S Model, to diagnose the various efforts of the excellent companies. The model focused on the so called 'hard' and 'soft' aspects of management effort. Up until then it was felt that the hard S's – strategy, structure and systems-dominated management thinking. What Peters and Waterman did was to make everyone aware of the soft S's – shared values, style of management, skills and staff. They attacked the prevailing business logic of hard numbers and analysis, and instead announced a passionate mandate that was based on People, Customers and Action.

Also central to the book was the concept of seven key attributes of the so called excellent companies and these encompassed:

1. **A bias for action**, active decision-making – 'getting on with it'.

2. **Close to the customer** – learning from the people served by the business.

3. **Autonomy and entrepreneurship** – fostering innovation and nurturing 'champions'.

4. **Productivity through people** – treating rank and file employees as a source of quality.

5. **Hands-on, value-driven** – management philosophy that guides everyday practice – management showing its commitment.

6. **Stick to the knitting** – stay with the business that you know.

7. **Simple form, lean staff** – some of the best companies have minimal HQ staff.

8. **Simultaneous loose-tight properties** – autonomy in shop-floor activities plus centralized values.

Today, Peters readily admits that some of the data in the study was flawed but nonetheless its effect was revolutionary.

Peters mandate is always about challenge and the pursuit of the new. He has often criticized the conventional approaches to strategy and indeed management; and takes great stock in mocking the political and game playing behaviours that characterize so much management behaviour in major corporations. Peters' language and ideas are always colourful and deliberately provocative. For him leadership is all about transformation.

> "The transforming leader is concerned with minutiae, as well. But he is concerned with a different kind of minutiae; he is concerned with the tricks of the pedagogue, the mentor, the linguist – the more successfully to become the value shaper, the exemplar, the maker of meanings. His job is much tougher than that of the transactional leader, for he is the true artist, the true pathfinder."

In *Thriving on Chaos* he wrote about the Master Paradox where all leaders at all levels must create internal stability in order to encourage the pursuit of constant change. Peters suggests that this paradox can be managed. He argues that people and leaders who can deal with paradox should be promoted. "An ability to embrace new ideas, routinely challenge old ones, and live with paradox will be the effective leader's premier trait." Like our other gurus, Peters advocates leaders who are visible and who "train, coach, cajole, care and comfort their staff". They are also responsible for creating excitement and loyalty by continually highlighting their colleagues' accomplishments. He is also keen to demolish the 'excessive vertical processing' of information in organizations – he advocates the principle of simple two page reporting. Urgency and creating an organization culture where change is the norm are vital leadership goals. A sense of urgency is ultimately created by individuals energetically testing, changing and improving.

Warren Bennis once said, "If Peter Drucker invented modern management, Tom Peters vivified it". It is the energy and radical fervour of Tom Peters that has set him apart from all other gurus. Whilst he has always had much to say on leadership, Peters' work has encompassed all aspect of the world of business and organizations including service, innovation, creativity and structure. His presentations and lectures are a tour de force of energy and radical challenge to all that is conventional. He has always tended to reject the analytical and rational side to leadership and management, and has instead focused on passion, enthusiasm and even fanaticism when it comes to leading organizations.

In October 2003, Peters released *Re-imagine! Business Excellence in a Disruptive Age*; a revolutionary coffee table sized book. It became an immediate international bestseller and, in keeping with Peters style, aims to do no less than re-invent the business book market.

Essential reading

Peters followed *In Search of Excellence* with a string of international bestsellers:

- *A Passion for Excellence*, with Nancy Austin, Collins London, 1985

- *Thriving on Chaos*, Macmillan, 1987

- *Liberation Management*, acclaimed as the 'Management Book of the Decade' for the '90s, 1992

- *The Tom Peters Seminar: Crazy Times Call for Crazy Organizations*, Vintage Books, 1994

- *The Pursuit of WOW!: Every Person's Guide to Topsy-The Project 50 and The Professional Service Firm 50* Vintage Books, 1994

WJ Reddin – Three Dimensional Leadership Grid

WJ (Bill) Reddin was one of the best known and respected authors in the UK during the 1970s and '80s. Born in the UK, he graduated from Harvard Business School and was subsequently a Sloan Doctorial Fellow at the Massachusetts Institute of Technology.

What is he famous for?

Bill Reddin is best known for the 3-D theory of management.

Reddin developed his idea from Blake and Mouton and detailed an eight box model of management behaviour. The grid is described in the classic terms of either relationship or task focused behaviour. Reddin's contribution over and above the Blake and Mouton Grid was his assertion that managerial behaviour can be positive or negative in any given situation. A major breakthrough of the theory was the acceptance that delegation was appropriate only in specific situations and that it was essentially hands-off in nature. He showed his ideas as sets of boxes in perspective, hence the name 3-D Grid.

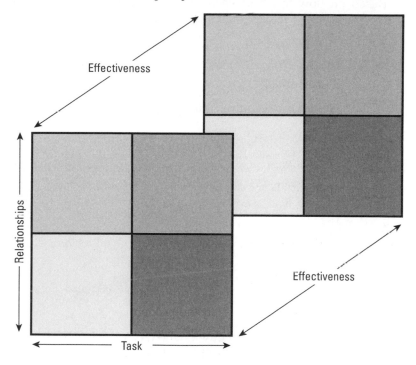

Reddin's three dimensions comprised:

- **Task Orientation** – the extent to which a manager directs their peoples' efforts towards goal accomplishment; behaviour characterized by planning, organizing and controlling. This dimension is about the quality of wanting to get a job done.

- **Relationships Orientation** – the extent to which a manager has personal relationships; behaviour characterized by mutual trust, respect for others' ideas and a consideration for their feelings. This dimension is about the quality of being interested primarily in people.

- **Effectiveness** – the extent to which a manager achieves the results requirements of their position –This dimension is about the ability to attain high productivity.

Based on how much of each of these characteristics a manager possesses, eight types of leadership style can be identified. Reddin described these types as:

- The Deserter, who has none or only a minimum of the three characteristics.

- The Bureaucrat, who has effectiveness only.

- The Missionary, who only has a relationship orientation.

- The Developer, who has both effectiveness and relationship orientations.

- The Autocrat, who only has a task orientation.

- The Benevolent Autocrat, who has both effectiveness and task orientations.

- The Compromiser, who has both task and relationship orientations.

- The Manager (Executive), who has all three characteristics.

Reddin's research led him to argue that the degree of relationship and task orientation were independent of effectiveness. In effect, either could be correlated with success depending on the given situation. As Reddin said:

> *"Some managers have learned that to be effective they must sometimes create an atmosphere which will induce self-motivation among their subordinates, and sometimes act in ways that appear either hard or soft. At other times, they must quietly efface themselves for a while and appear to do nothing. It would seem more accurate to say, then, that any basic style of management may be used more or less effectively, depending upon the situation."*

Reddin's model is a conceptual framework that develops three essential managerial skills:

1. **Diagnostic skills** – the ability to evaluate a situation.

2. **Flexibility of style** – the ability to match a managerial approach to a given situation.

3. **Situational management** – the ability to change a situation needing to be changed.

A clear set of indicators and characteristics for each type was developed that enables each style to be understood.

In showing that any of the four basic styles of behaviour could be effective in some situations and ineffective in others, he produced his eight distinctive managerial styles around his notion of effectiveness.

BASIC STYLE	LESS EFFECTIVE STYLE	MORE EFFECTIVE STYLE
Integrated	Compromiser	Executive Manager
Dedicated	Autocrat	Benevolent Autocrat
Related	Missionary	Developer
Separated	Deserter	Bureaucrat

Here is a summary of the main characteristics of each of the eight styles:

Less Effective			
DESERTER	**MISSIONARY**	**AUTOCRAT**	**COMPROMISER**
Uninvolved	Easy going	Tough	Blows with the wind
Lowers morale	Helpful	Dictatorial	Indecisive
Invisible	Weak	Stubborn	Short-term orientation
More Effective			
BUREAUCRAT	**DEVELOPER**	**BENEVOLENT AUTOCRAT**	**MANAGER (EXECUTIVE)**
Follows rules	Creative	Smooth	High standards
Organization person	Delegates well	Organizer	Motivates well
Disinterest Camouflaged	Trusting	Self-committed	Long-term orientation

Managerial effectiveness is measured by the extent to which a manager achieves the output of a task or job. Reddin argued that it was critical that instead of focusing on inputs, managers needed to work on achieving outputs.

Some of his observations included:

"Effectiveness is the central issue in management. It is the manager's job to be effective, it is the only job."

"Energy is often confused with effectiveness."

"Too many managers want to be clever, rather than effective."

"Chief Executive Officers could be assessed according to the amount of time they could remain dead in their office with no one noticing. If a long time, it means they are concentrating long range decisions, which is what they are being paid for."

Essential reading

- *Managerial Effectiveness*, New York, McGraw Hill, 1970

- *The Best of Bill Reddin*, IPM, 1985

- *How to Make Managerial Style More Effective*, McGraw Hill, Maidenhead,1987

Tannenbaum and Schmidt – The leadership continuum

What are they famous for?

The Tannenbaum and Schmidt Continuum is another simple but classic leadership model that shows the relationship between the level of freedom a manager chooses to give to a team, and the level of authority they use. Their continuum model uses a simple diagram that illustrates the range of possible behaviours available to any leader. Each type of action is related to the degree of authority exercised by the leader and the amount of freedom people are allowed in taking decisions. As a team's freedom is increased, so the manager's authority decreases. This, Tannenbaum and Schmidt argued was a very positive and useful way for both teams and managers to develop.

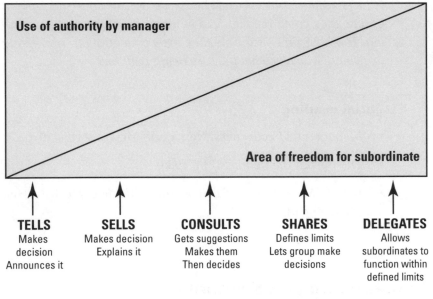

TELLS	**SELLS**	**CONSULTS**	**SHARES**	**DELEGATES**
Makes decision Announces it	Makes decision Explains it	Gets suggestions Makes them Then decides	Defines limits Lets group make decisions	Allows subordinates to function within defined limits

*Continuum of leadership behaviour
(Tannenbaum & Schmidt, Harvard Business School)*

Tannenbaum and Schmidt argued that three factors have to be considered by any leader:

1. **Manager Forces** – These are described as the forces operating as a result of our own personality.

2. **Subordinate Forces** – How as managers or leaders we are influenced by others expectations and personalities.

3. **Situational Forces** – These are the critical external pressures impacting on a leader – which might come from the actual task, organization, work group or time pressures.

In their basic thesis Tannenbaum and Schmidt concluded that there are two key issues to consider. The first is that a successful leader is one who is acutely aware of these forces and their relevant to their behaviour at any given time. Successful leaders clearly understand themselves, their people, organization and the broader social business environment in which they operate. The second issue is that the successful leader is able to behave appropriately in the light of these perceptions. If direction is needed, they are able to direct; if participative freedom is called for, they are able to provide such freedom.

They defined the seven leadership behaviours or levels as follows:

1. THE MANAGER DECIDES AND ANNOUNCES THE DECISION

The manager reviews options in light of aims, issues, priorities and timescales, and then decides the action to be taken before informing the team of the decision. The manager will probably have considered how the team will react, but the team plays no active part in making the decision. The team may perceive the manager as not taking the team's welfare into account. This is seen by the team as a purely task-based decision.

2. THE MANAGER DECIDES AND THEN 'SELLS' THE DECISION TO THE GROUP

The manager makes the decision as in 1 above, and then explains the reasons for the decision to the team. They stress the positive benefits that the team will enjoy from the decision. In so doing, the manager or leader is seen by the team as recognizing the team's importance and having some concern for the team.

3. THE MANAGER PRESENTS THE DECISION WITH BACKGROUND IDEAS AND INVITES QUESTIONS

The manager presents the decision, along with some of the background information that resulted in the decision. The team is invited to ask questions and discuss the reasons behind the decision. This approach enables the team to understand and accept or agree with the decision. As a more participative and involving approach it enables the team to appreciate the issues and reasons for the decision, and the implications of the various options involved. This will have a more motivational approach than 1 or 2 because of the higher level of team involvement and open discussion.

4. THE MANAGER SUGGESTS A PROVISIONAL DECISION AND INVITES DISCUSSION ABOUT IT

The manager reviews a provisional decision with the team on the basis that they will take into account some of the views before making a final decision. This allows the team to have some real influence over the shape of the manager's final decision. This leadership approach acknowledges that the team has something to contribute to the decision-making process, as such it is a more involving and motivational style than the previous level.

5. THE MANAGER PRESENTS THE SITUATION OR PROBLEM OBTAINS SUGGESTIONS AND THEN DECIDES

The manager presents the situation, and provides some options. The team is then encouraged and expected to offer ideas and additional options which are then discussed along with the implications of each possible course of action. The manager then decides which option to take. This level is one of high involvement for the team, and is appropriate when the team has more detailed knowledge or experience of the issues than the manager. Using a very high level of involvement and influence this approach provides more motivation and freedom than any of the previous levels.

6. THE MANAGER EXPLAINS THE SITUATION DEFINES THE PARAMETERS AND ASKS THE TEAM TO DECIDE

At this level the manager has effectively delegated responsibility for the decision to the team within stated limits. The manager may or may not choose to be a part of the team which decides. While this approach appears to gives a huge responsibility to the team, the manager can control the risk and outcomes to an extent, according to any constraints they might outline at the beginning of the task. This highly motivational level requires a mature team for any serious situation or problem.

7. THE MANAGER ALLOWS THE TEAM TO IDENTIFY THE PROBLEM, DEVELOP THE OPTIONS AND DECIDE ON THE ACTION, WITHIN THE MANAGER'S RECEIVED LIMITS

This is obviously the extreme end of delegated freedom, whereby the team is effectively doing what the manager did in level 1. The team is given responsibility for identifying and analyzing the situation or problem; developing and assessing all possible options; evaluating the various options and implications, and deciding on and implementing a specific course of action.

The manager also states in advance that they will support the decision and help the team implement it. The manager may or may not be part of the team, and if so then they have no more authority than anyone else in the team. The only constraints and parameters for the team are the ones that the manager had imposed on them from their boss(es). Again, the manager retains accountability for any resulting problems, while the team must get the credit for any successes. This level is potentially the most motivational of all, but also potentially the most dangerous. Not surprisingly, the team must be mature and competent, and capable of acting with the relevant responsibilities.

So the model promotes the idea that any successful leader accurately assesses the forces to determine the most appropriate leadership behaviour at any given time. By possessing this level of insight and demonstrating appropriate flexibility, a leader is less likely to see leadership as full of dilemmas and more as a positive challenge.

The Tannenbaum and Schmidt model remains a classic description of leadership styles and is frequently cited when helping people to explore the range of leadership options available.

Essential reading

- *How to Choose a Leadership Pattern*, Harvard Business Review, May/June, 1973

Abraham Zaleznik – Leadership versus management

Abraham Zaleznik is the Konosuke Matsushita Professor of Leadership, Emeritus at the Harvard Business School. Harvard Business School awarded him the MBA degree with distinction in 1947 and the Doctor of Commercial Science degree in 1951. Zaleznik began his career at Harvard as a research assistant and became a full professor in 1962 and was inaugurated with the Cahners-Rabb professorship in social psychology of management.

In 1960, Professor Zaleznik became a candidate in psychoanalysis at the Boston Psychoanalytic Institute, one of the affiliate institutes of the American Psychoanalytic Association. He was granted a waiver of medical and psychiatric pre-requisites and graduated as a clinical psychoanalyst in 1968. In 1971, Professor Zaleznik received certification for the practice of psychoanalysis from the American Psychoanalytic Association. His objective in undertaking psychoanalytic training was to prepare himself for specialized research and teaching in the psychodynamics of leadership and group psychology.

In 1982, Zaleznik, along with his colleague Professor C. Roland Christensen, travelled to Japan to Konosuke Matsushita, the founder of the famed Matsushita Electric Company. As a result of this meeting in Osaka, Mr. Matsushita pledged the funds to the Harvard Business School to establish a chair in leadership, the first gift to an American university of its kind. Harvard University elected Zaleznik to this chair, from which he taught The Psychodynamics of Leadership and continued his research on leadership. In recognition of his 43 years on the Faculty, the Harvard Business School Alumni Association awarded him the Distinguished Service Award in 1996.

During his career at the Harvard Business School, he authored or co-authored 14 books and numerous articles. His *Harvard Business Review* article entitled, 'Managers and Leaders: Are They Different?' received the McKinsey award for the best *Harvard Business Review* article in 1977 and was re-published as a classic in 1992. Earlier and later articles received the same recognition.

Extending his clinical practice of psychoanalysis, Professor Zaleznik has engaged in consulting work on organizational planning, succession and in the resolution of conflict in organizations. Since 1970, he has served on many corporate boards. Currently, he serves on six boards of privately and publicly held corporations. In addition to his consulting practice, he continues to write.

What is he famous for?

"Leadership is made of substance, humanity and morality and we are painfully short of all three qualities in our collective lives."

A running theme throughout this book has been the concern of our gurus to distinguish between leadership and management. In 1977, Zaleznik wrote a classic article in the *Harvard Business Review* entitled 'Managers and Leaders are they Different?" The article set out some distinctive characteristics between leaders and managers.

Zaleznik made the point that leaders are people who energize organizations that are often associated with chaos. "No matter how much you plan, when you get to the workplace there are unanticipated problems." In contrast, managers are concerned with ensuring the stability of the organization. He put forward the notion that leaders are generally more comfortable with ambiguity and that they provide a critical dynamic to organization success. To some extent he was an early originator of the notion of transformational leadership that has since been popularized by people like Kotter.

> *"One often hears leaders referred to with adjectives rich in emotional content. Leaders attract strong feelings of identity and differences of love and hate. Human relations in leader-dominated structures often appear turbulent, intense and at times even disorganized. Such an atmosphere intensifies individual motivation and often produces unanticipated outcomes."*

He argued that we have a longing for great leaders but also a need for competent managers. He went on to distinguish differences between the two.

"What it takes to develop managers may inhibit developing leaders."

For Zaleznik management is all about operating in a culture that "emphasizes rationality and control". He went on to argue that in this type of environment and organization "it takes neither genius or nor heroism to be a manager, but rather persistence, tough mindedness, hard work, intelligence, analytical ability and, perhaps most important, tolerance and goodwill".

He also asserts that "another conception of leadership ... attaches almost mystical beliefs to what a leader is and assumes that only great people are worthy of the drama of power and politics. Here leadership is a psychodrama in which a brilliant, lonely person must gain control for himself or herself as a precondition for controlling others. Such an exception of leadership contrasts sharply with the mundane, practical and yet important conception that leadership is really managing work that other people do".

Zaleznik summed up the dilemma between leadership and management as "what it takes to ensure a supply of people who will assume practical responsibility may inhibit the development of great leaders. On the other hand, the presence of great leaders may undermine the development of managers who typically become very anxious in the relative disorder that leaders seem to generate".

When it comes to developing leaders and managers, Zaleznik argued that the latter are developed by a process of socialization that prepares them to "guide institutions and maintain the existing balance of social relations". Leaders he believed are developed through "personal mastery which impels an individual to struggle for psychological and social change".

The effect of Zaleznik's article was to raise the level of debate around what organizations were doing in terms of developing leadership. It also stimulated further thinking around the wider leadership debate. Today his ideas seemed to be ahead of their time when we reflect on the recent writings of Kotter and Kouzes and Posner, who argue for transformational leadership.

Essential reading

- *Managers and Leaders: Are they Different?*, Harvard Business Review, May, June 1977

- *The Managerial Mystique: Restoring Leadership in Business*, New York, Harper and Row Publishers, 1989

THREE
The leadership tool box

Some thoughts on leadership and managing

The following chapter provides a wide range of miscellaneous quotes, checklists and ideas involving the concept of management and leadership. Use it to stimulate your own thinking and ideas. Perhaps the ideas might help you to reflect on your own leadership style and approach, or provide some stimulus for a discussion with colleagues or a presentation of some kind.

Leadership – a test case of adversity

Few great leaders encountered defeats so consistently before enjoying ultimate victory as did this individual. A frequently reported listing of these failures includes the following:

Failed in business in 1831

▼

Ran for the legislature and lost in 1832

▼

Failed once again in business in 1834

▼

Sweetheart died in 1835

▼

Had a nervous breakdown in 1836

▼

Lost a second political race in 1838

▼

Defeated for Congress in 1843

▼

Defeated for Congress in 1846

▼

Defeated for Congress in 1848

▼

Defeated for US Senate in 1855

▼

Defeated for Vice-President in 1856

▼

Defeated for US Senate in 1858

The man was Abraham Lincoln who was elected sixteenth President of the United States in 1860.

Leadership attributes

John Gardner studied a large number of organizations and leaders and concluded that there were some qualities and attributes that did appear to point to a set of generic attributes:

- Physical vitality and stamina

- Intelligence and action oriented judgement

- Eagerness to accept responsibility

- Task competence

- Understanding of followers and their needs

- Skills in dealing with people

- Need for achievement

- Capacity to motivate people

- Courage and resolution

- Trustworthiness

- Decisiveness

- Self-confidence

- Assertiveness

- Adaptability/ Flexibility

John Gardner, *On Leadership, New York Free Press, 1989.*

The leader and change

Warren Bennis, *while president of the University of Cincinnati.*

"My moment of truth came toward the end of my first ten months. It was one of those nights in the office. The clock was moving toward four in the morning, and I was still not through with the incredible mass of paper stacked before me. I was bone weary and soul weary, and I found myself muttering, 'either I can't manage this place, or it's unmanageable'. I reached for my calendar and ran my eyes down each hour, half-hour, and quarter-hour to see where my time had gone that day, the day before, the month before... My discovery was this: I had become the victim of a vast, amorphous, unwitting, unconscious conspiracy to prevent me from doing anything whatever to change the university's status quo."

How to be an outstanding manager

"Good managers realize that the difference between them and others in the business lies in the transition they have made from completing jobs and tasks themselves to 'getting things done through others'. Whatever the manager achieves has a multiplier effect. If she or he gets it right, others will get it right. If he or she screws it up, others will screw it up.

I find myself intolerant of management books that seek to prescribe exactly 'how it should be done'. My own experience shows that there are many different ways of achieving one's aims and many different ways of leading an industrial company. I have worked with leaders whose style is so totally different to my own that I have found it incomprehensible that they achieve results, but nevertheless they do. Each one of us has to develop our own style, and our own approach, using such skills and personal qualities as we have inherited... My own experience of trying to teach and train managers is that it is extremely difficult to teach grown-up people anything. It is, however, relatively easy to create conditions under which people will teach themselves. Indeed, most people wish to improve their own performance and are eager to do so. That is why there are so many books on management published and that is why I have read practically all of them. As I said earlier, too many make impossible promises and claims for no one can manage or lead in someone else's clothes. What each of us does over a long period of trial and error is to acquire a set of tools with which we are comfortable and which we can apply in different ways to the myriad problems which we need to solve."

John Harvey-Jones
Former Chief Executive and Chairman of ICI
Making it Happen

"There is a difference between leadership and management. The leader and those who follow represent one of the oldest, most natural and most effective human relationships. The manager and those managed are a later product with neither so romantic or inspiring history. Leadership is the spirit, compounded by personality and vision – its practice is an art. Management is of the mind, more a matter of accurate calculation, statistics, methods, timetables and routine – its practice is a science."

Marshall Sir William Slim

Positive rules for leaders who want to achieve excellent results

1. Involve all relevant people from the start.

2. Have a single, fully worked out object in view – aim to kill one bird with many stones, not two birds with one.

3. Having obtained the best possible information and counsel in concert, act on it, in concert.

4. Be governed by what you know, rather than what you fear.

5. Embody the decisions in a comprehensive plan that everybody knows and that will cover the expected consequences of setback or success.

6. Entrust the plan's execution to competent people with no conflicting responsibilities.

7. Leave operational people to operate.

8. In the event of serious failure, start again to review and renew the decisions.

9. Only abandon the decision when it is plain to all that the objectives cannot be achieved.

Robert Heller, *The Decision Makers*

Thriving on chaos – Tom Peters

1. The best and brightest people will gravitate towards those corporations that foster personal growth.

2. The manager's new role is that of coach, teacher and mentor.

3. The best people want ownership – psychic and literal – in a company; the best companies are providing it.

4. Companies will increasingly turn to third-party contractors, shifting from hired labour to contract labour.

5. Authoritarian management is yielding to a networking, people style of management.

6. Entrepreneurship within corporations – intrapreneurship – is creating new products and new markets and revitalizing companies inside out.

7. Quality will be paramount.

8. Intuition and creativity are challenging the 'it's all in the numbers' business school philosophy.

9. Large corporations are emulating the positive and productive qualities of small business.

10. The dawn of the information economy has fostered a massive shift from infrastructure to quality of life.

Selected from his best selling work *Thriving on Chaos*.

The generosity of a great leader

Nelson Mandela, shortly after the end of apartheid, delivered a speech that showed immense generosity and humility in the face of the struggles he had faced in life. It demonstrated his uniqueness as a leader.

"I would like to take this opportunity to thank the world leaders who have given messages of support. I would also congratulate Mr FW De Klerk for the four years that we have worked together, quarrelled, addressed sensitive problems and at the end of our heated exchanges were able to shake hands and to drink coffee.

To the people of South Africa and the world who are watching, the election has been a triumph for the human spirit.

South Africa's heroes are legends across the generations. But it is the people who are true heroes. The election victory is one of the most important moments in the life of South Africa. I am proud of the ordinary, humble people of South Africa who have shown calm, patient determination to reclaim South Africa, and joy that we can loudly proclaim from the rooftops – free at last!

I intend to be a servant not a leader; as one above others. I pledge to use all my strength and ability to live up to the world's expectations of me."

Nelson Mandela

Personal effectiveness for leaders

Check yourself against this programme once a month for the next six months. Protect your most valuable commodity – time:

DEVELOP A NEW PERSONAL SENSE OF TIME

- Do not rely on memory; record where your time goes.

PLAN AHEAD

- Make plans on how you are going to spend your time a day, a week, a month and one year ahead. Plan your time in terms of opportunities and results, priorities and deadlines.

MAKE THE MOST OF YOUR BEST TIME

- Programme important tasks for the time of day you function best. Have planned quiet periods for creative thinking.

CAPITALIZE ON MARGINAL TIME

- Squeeze activities into the minutes you spend waiting for a train or between meetings.

AVOID CLUTTER

- Try re-organizing your desk for effectiveness. Sort papers into categories according to action priorities. Generate as little paper as possible yourself.

DO IT NOW

- `Procrastination is the thief of time'.
- `My object was always to do the business of the day in the day' – Lord Wellington.

LEARN TO SAY 'NO'

- Do not let others misappropriate your time.
- Decline tactfully but firmly to avoid over-commitment.

USE THE TELEPHONE AS A TIME-SAVING TOOL

- Keep telephone calls down to minimum length.
- Screen telephone interruptions.

- Learn to delegate as much as possible.

- Keep them short.

- Sharpen your skills as a chairperson.

- Cut out unnecessary meetings.

John Adair, *Effective Leadership*

Leadership and change

"And one should bear in mind that there is nothing more difficult to execute, nor more dubious of success, nor more dangerous to administer than to introduce a new order of things; for he who introduces it has all those who profit from the old order as his enemies, and he has only lukewarm allies in all those who might profit from the new. This luke-warmness partly stems from fear of their adversaries who have the law on their side, and partly from scepticism of men, who do not truly believe in new things unless they have actually had personal experience of them. Therefore, it happens that whenever those who are enemies have the chance to attack, they do so enthusiastically, whereas those others defend hesitantly, so that they, together with the prince, are in danger."

Nicolo Machiavelli, *The Prince.*

Leadership and cost control

There are several prerequisites for effective cost control:

1. **Concentration must centre on controlling the costs where they are**. It takes approximately as much effort to cut 10% off a cost item of $50,000 as it does to cut 10% off a cost item of $5 million. Costs, too, in other words are a social phenomenon, with 90% or so of the costs incurred by 10% or so of the activities.

2. **Different costs must be treated differently**. Costs vary enormously in their character – as do products.

3. **The one truly effective way to cut costs is to cut out an activity altogether**. To try to cut back costs is rarely effective. There is little point in trying to do cheaply what should not be done at all. Typically, however, the cost-cutting drive starts with a declaration by management that no activity or department is to be demolished. This condemns the whole exercise to futility. It can only result in harming essential activities – and in making sure that the unessential ones will be back at their full, original cost level within a few months.

4. **Effective control of costs requires that the whole business be looked at** – just as all the result areas of a business have to be looked at to gain understanding. Otherwise, costs will be reduced in one place by simply being pushed somewhere else. This looks like a great victory for cost reduction – until the final results are in a few months later, with total costs being as high as ever. There is, for example, the cost reduction in manufacturing which is achieved by pushing the burden of adjustment onto the shipping-room and warehouse. There is the cost reduction of inventory which pushes the costs of uncontrolled fluctuation upstream onto manufacturing. There is, typically, a great cost reduction in the price of some purchased material which, however, results in longer, slower and costlier machine work to handle the less than perfect substitute material. These examples, as every manager knows, could be continued almost ad infinitum.

5. **Cost is a term of economics**. The cost system that needs to be analyzed is therefore the entire economic activity which produces economic value.

Peter Drucker, *Managing For Results*

Differentiating leading from managing

Throughout this book you will have read of distinctions between managing and leading. Consider your own preferences in relation to the following

1. Leadership is an art – *Management is a science*

2. Leaders lead people – *Managers manage things*

3. Leaders operate in the future – *Managers deal in the present*

4. Leaders are agents of change – *Managers deal with the status-quo*

5. Leaders empower – *Managers' control*

6. Leaders strive for effectiveness – *Managers aim for efficiency*

7. Leaders inspire – *Managers seek compliance*

8. Leaders listen – *Manager talk*

9. Leaders make people feel strong – *Managers' direct people*

10. Leaders stretch people – *Managers maintain people*

11. Leaders excite people – *Managers monitor people*

12. Leaders defy order – *Managers seek order*

13. Leaders make time – *Managers are busy*

14. Leaders experiment – *Managers create routines*

15. Leaders create institutions – *Managers run them*

Leadership styles

Discussion Generator – a personal perspective on some leaders and their styles – Where would you place people on your list?

CHARISMATIC LEADERS	AUTOCRATIC/ ASSERTIVE LEADERS	DEMOCRATIC LEADERS
General De Gaulle	Margaret Thatcher	John Major
Mrs Gandi	Francois Mitterrand	Bill Clinton
John F Kennedy	Richard Nixon	George Bush Snr
General Franco	V. Giscard d'Estaing	Anita Roddick
Bill Clinton	George W Bush	Richard Branson
Napoleon	Lou Gerstener	Lucianno Bennetton
Jack Welch	Alex Ferguson	John Brown
Richard Branson	Robert Maxwell	David Sainsbury
Ronald Reagan	John Birt	Sir John Harvey Jones
Mikhail Gorbachev	Vladimir Putin	
Winston Churchill	Lord King	
Ataturk	Sir Richard Greenbury	
Bill Gates	Al Dunlap	
Lee Iacocca	Tony Blair	
Sir John Harvey Jones		
John Chambers		
Elliot Spitzer		
Nelson Mandela		
Mahatma Ghandi		

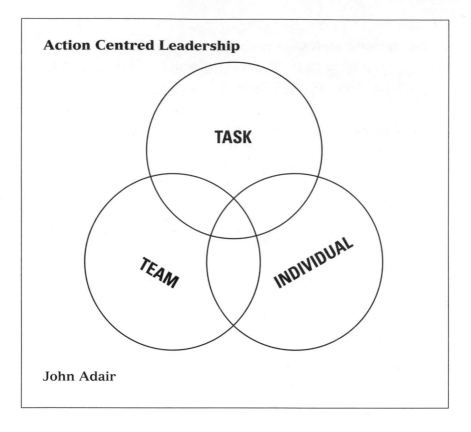

Action Centred Leadership

TASK

TEAM

INDIVIDUAL

John Adair

Checklist for meeting individual needs

1 Have I agreed with each of my team their key responsibilities and required standards of performance?

2 Does my team have all the resources necessary to achieve their key tasks (including sufficient authority)?

3 Have I made provision for the training and development of team members?

4   Do I praise excellent performance? In the case of average performance, do I criticize constructively and provide, where appropriate, help and guidance?

5   Have I achieved the right balance between controlling and letting go?

7   Could I delegate additional authority? For example, could Sam arrange the project review meeting and run it? Could James take on some of my existing reporting relationships?

8   Do I engage in regular team and individual performance reviews?

9   Do I know enough about each team member to enable me to have an accurate understanding of their individual needs, strengths and development needs?

Checklist for achieving the task

1   Am I clear about my own responsibilities and authority? Have I agreed this with my boss?

2   Am I clear about the objectives of my team/unit?

3   Have I worked out an action plan for reaching these objectives and discussed it with my team?

4   Is the team sufficiently capable? Could the team be restructured to deliver better results?

5   Does everyone know exactly what their role and key responsibilities are? Does each team member have clearly defined and agreed performance targets?

6   Is anyone over-loaded or insufficiently allocated a workload?

7   Are the lines of authority and accountability clear within the team?

8   Are there any capability gaps in the team (including me) that might prevent us achieving our goals? If so, what are my plans for addressing these gaps?

9   Are we focused on the right priorities?

10 Do I receive regular information that enables me to check progress?

11 Do I regularly review performance? Have I achieved the tasks set twelve months ago?

12 Does my work and behaviour set the best possible example to the team?

Checklist for maintaining the team

1   Do I set team objectives with members and ensure that everyone understands them?

2   Is the team clear as to the working standards expected, e.g. in time keeping, quality of work, procedures? Am I fair and impartial in enforcing the rules? Is the team aware of the consequences of infringement (penalties)?

3   Is the size of the team correct and are the right people working together? Is there a need for new teams to be developed?

4   Do I look for opportunities for building teamwork into tasks?

5   Do I take action on matters likely to disrupt the team, e.g. unjustified differentials in reward, uneven workloads?

6   Is the grievance procedure understood by all? Do I deal with all grievances and complaints promptly?

7   Do I welcome and encourage new ideas and suggestions from the team?

8   Do I provide regular opportunities for genuine discussion of the team before taking decisions affecting them, e.g. decisions relating to work plans, work methods and standards?

9   Do I regularly brief the team (e.g. monthly) on the organization's plans and any future developments?

10 Is the overall performance of each individual regularly (e.g. annually) reviewed?

11 Am I sure that, for individual work, capability and reward are in balance?

12 If after opportunities for training and development, an individual is still not meeting the requirements of the job, do I try and find a position for them which matches their capacity – or see that someone else does?

13 Do I know enough about the members of the team to enable me to have an accurate picture of their needs, aptitudes and attitudes? Do I really know how they feel about things?

14 Do I give sufficient time and personal attention to matters of direct concern to team members?

Leading high performing teams

This checklist is designed to help you think about the behaviours your leadership style might be generating in your team. Read over the scales and mark the behaviours of your team. What do the results say about how you may be exercising your leadership role?

1. Listening skills amongst the team

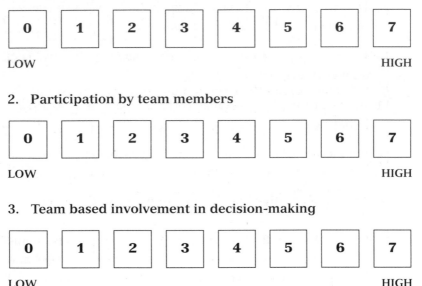

| 0 | 1 | 2 | 3 | 4 | 5 | 6 | 7 |

LOW   HIGH

2. Participation by team members

| 0 | 1 | 2 | 3 | 4 | 5 | 6 | 7 |

LOW   HIGH

3. Team based involvement in decision-making

| 0 | 1 | 2 | 3 | 4 | 5 | 6 | 7 |

LOW   HIGH

4. Building and developing on individual contributions

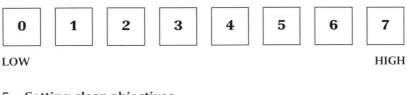

| 0 | 1 | 2 | 3 | 4 | 5 | 6 | 7 |

LOW   HIGH

5. Setting clear objectives

| 0 | 1 | 2 | 3 | 4 | 5 | 6 | 7 |

LOW   HIGH

6. Managing time and priorities

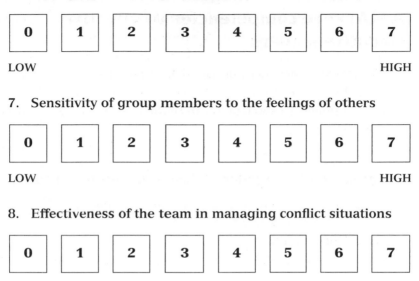

| 0 | 1 | 2 | 3 | 4 | 5 | 6 | 7 |

LOW   HIGH

7. Sensitivity of group members to the feelings of others

| 0 | 1 | 2 | 3 | 4 | 5 | 6 | 7 |

LOW   HIGH

8. Effectiveness of the team in managing conflict situations

| 0 | 1 | 2 | 3 | 4 | 5 | 6 | 7 |

LOW   HIGH

9. Levels of creativity and innovation within the team

| 0 | 1 | 2 | 3 | 4 | 5 | 6 | 7 |

LOW   HIGH

The American Management Association's (AMA) core competencies of effective executive leaders

The American Management Association have developed a list of core competencies needed for effective executive leadership. The model was developed in association with Dr John Nichols a UK based leadership consultant.

The *strategic* competency: *Leading with the head*

Think, plan and organize analytically *and* intuitively.

TYPICAL BEHAVIOURS

- Creates a clear vision of what is to be accomplished

- Develops strategies and plans

- Uses intuition imaginatively

- Understands today in terms of the big picture and identifies trends

- Balances the short with the long term

- Is logical and planful

- Is open minded and receptive to new ideas

- Tackles complex problems creatively

- Is decisive, but flexible

The *performance management* competency: *Leading with the hands*

Orchestrate an effective organizational or team effort to achieve the desired results.

TYPICAL BEHAVIOURS

- Sets a clear direction and challenging goals

- Assigns roles and responsibilities

- Matches style to individuals and situations

- Coaches, empowers and delegates where appropriate

- Gives timely praise and corrective feedback as appropriate

- Recognizes people and rewards them for their achievements

- Confronts and improves poor performance; disciplines when necessary

- Handles crises; identifies and resolves conflicts

- Represents and advocates for the organization/team

- Builds a cohesive team of people working together towards common goals

- Leads change, brings people with them, overcomes resistance

The *inspirational* competency: *Leading with the heart*

Enlist, energize and empower others to struggle to achieve shared goals through effective communication of the vision, commitment to demonstrated values and the use of positive power and influence.

TYPICAL BEHAVIOURS

- Communicates an inspiring vision that grabs attention

- Promotes open, wideband, interactive communication

- Understands others, their *values, aspirations, needs* and *desires*, and pitches messages accordingly

- Expresses self confidently and assertively but not aggressively

- Influences through the use of positive power and influences using negotiation, involvement, direction and example

- Uses power mostly with restraint and tact – but quickly and assuredly when necessary

- Satisfies the security, status and social needs of others

- Provides meaning for people and inspires enthusiasm about ideas and efforts

- Shapes a high-achievement culture where work is meaning-ful, interesting and challenging

The *character* competency: *Leading through trust*

Conduct yourself in a responsible, ethical way that earns trust.

TYPICAL BEHAVIOURS

- Acts ethically, with integrity

- Upholds values and principles that create a climate of trust and integrity

- Demonstrates courage to take tough decisions in line with principles

- Keeps promises

- Accepts accountability for own actions and those of followers

- Sets a worthy example to others

We can summarize the different aspects of our AMA Leadership Model – what leaders do, the leadership process and the underlying compe-tencies – in the following model.

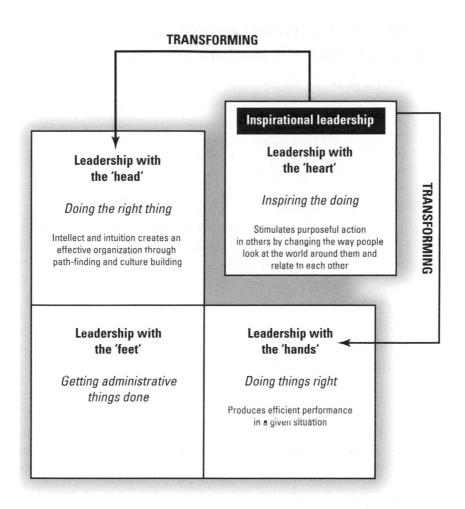

Inspirational leadership, from the heart,
transforms the way the leader leads ©AMA

Leadership skills and personal characteristics – A useful checklist

1. **Leadership** – Provides direction under uncertain conditions; has an intense 'desire to succeed' coupled with the perseverance and creativity to ensure success; has the ability to 'fire up' large audiences; communicates complex ideas in a simple and straightforward manner; is assertive; shows initiative; is driven to do an 'outrageously' good job.

2. **Strategic thinking** – Can deal with ideas at an abstract level; readily learns and understands concepts outside of his/her immediate functional area; has the ability to conceptualize 'what could be'; uses one's imagination in creating a vision that forms the basis for deciding on new concepts for which there is no data.

3. **Innovation and creativity** – Is perceptive, intuitive and creative. Sees more than the obvious when confronted with business situations and problems, rapidly identifying the implications; uses innovative approaches and leading edge technologies in solving problems.

4. **Risk taking and a 'bias for action'** – is willing to take personal risks to advance new ideas and programs for the success of the company; has the courage to commit sizeable resources based on a blend of analysis and intuition; is comfortable with making the percentages, rather than achieving success with each initiative; trusts own judgement and instincts without requiring definitive proof; prefers quick and approximate actions to slow and precise approaches.

5. **Decision-making** – Has the ability to make difficult, unpopular choices in order to achieve larger strategic objectives; constantly gathers and analyses information from others; is open to influence and change; demonstrates confidence, strength of conviction and sound judgement.

6. **Knowledge of field** – Has a fundamental understanding of ideas techniques, leading edge supplied technologies, trends and discoveries (both inside and outside the company) that pertain to assigned work responsibilities; seeks out and quickly understands new developments.

7. **Managerial proficiency** – Has a set of well-honed 'fundamental operating principles' to help guide goal-setting, problem identification and decision-making; has the capacity to drive a negotiation to closing without compromising away one's central requirements; understands complex operational issues quickly and takes appropriate action; executes well.

8. **Resourcefulness** – Adapts to rapidly changing conditions; learns from successes and failure; mediates differences; maintains a flexible and constructive orientation; buffers pressures received from others; demonstrates a high level of initiative, drive, persistence and involvement.

9. **Maturity and stability** – Has an accurate picture of strengths and areas for improvement; is willing to learn and improve; controls emotions; refrains from over-reacting.

10. **Communications** – Expresses ideas and concerns clearly and persuasively; is proficient and confident making formal presentations; participates easily and influentially in business meetings; has flexible and effective writing skills.

11. **Interpersonal competence** – Listens effectively; is sensitive to the needs of people; develops rapport and trust; gives criticism appropriately; solicits interpersonal feedback; is candid and direct in a constructive manner; accepts interpersonal differences.

Courtesy of Rank Xerox

FOUR
Leadership quotes

What some people have had to say about leadership

Leadership is making happen what wouldn't happen anyway and this always entails working at the edge of what is acceptable

Richard Pascale

Leadership is not rank, privileges, title or money. It is responsibility

Peter Drucker

The first responsibility of a leader is to define reality. The last is to say thank you. In between the two, the leader must become a servant and debtor

Max DePree

A good leader must be tough enough to win a fight, but not tough enough to kick a man when he is down

WG Bennis and EH Schein

Let us have faith that might makes right, and let us do our duty as we understand it

Abraham Lincoln

Leadership is the art of mobilising others to want to struggle for shared aspirations

James Kouzes and Barry Posner

Is there not a difference between good leaders and leaders for good?

John Lord

The speed of the boss is the speed of the team

Lee Iacocca

A leader is someone who knows what they want to achieve and can communicate that. But you will only succeed if you know what you are doing is right and you know how to bring out the best in people

Margaret Thatcher

Leaders should not be easily provoked

St Paul

You can buy a man's (person's) time, you can even buy his physical presence at a given place, but you cannot buy enthusiasm... You cannot buy loyalty... You cannot buy the devotion of hearts, minds, or souls. You must earn these

Charles Frances

The only interesting thing about leadership is the bit we can't define

George Braque

As you grow, hire people who are smarter than you are and then get them to sell your organization to new clients, not yourself. You cannot do it all

Mark McCormack

One of the simplest and most effective ways of distinguishing between the role of leadership and the function of management is to take authority out of the equation. If the manager did not have the authority to tell people what to do, would they still do what he or she wants them to?

W Goldsmith and D Clutterbuck

Take the course opposite to custom and you will almost always do well

Jean Jacques Rousseau

You will never be a leader unless you first learn to follow and be led

Tiorio

It's no exaggeration to say that a strong positive self-image is the best possible preparation for leadership in life

Dr. Joyce Brothers

The most self-conscious people in the world are its leaders. They may also be the most anxious and insecure. As men (people) of action, leaders face risks and uncertainty, and often display remarkable courage in shouldering brave responsibility. But beneath their fortitude, there often lies an agonizing sense of doubt and a need to justify themselves

Abraham Zaleznik

A leader is a man (person) who has the ability to get other people to do what they don't want to do and like it

Harry Truman

Coaches who can outline plays on the blackboard are a dime a dozen. The ones who succeed are those who can get inside their players and motivate them

Vince Lombardi

Leaders have a significant role in creating the state of mind that is the society. They can serve as symbols of the moral unity of the society. They can express the values that hold the society together. Most importantly, they can conceive and articulate goals that lift people out of their petty pre-occupations, carry them above the conflicts that tear a society apart, and unite them in the pursuit of objectives worthy of their best efforts

John Gardner

Example is not the main thing in influencing others. It is the only thing

Albert Schweitzer

Leadership is like the Abominable Snowman, whose footprints are everywhere but who is nowhere to be seen

Bennis & Nanus

There are almost as many definitions of leadership as there are persons who have attempted to define the concept

Stogdill

A leader is best when people barely know that he exists, not so good when people obey and acclaim him, worst when they despise him. 'Fail to honour people' they fail to honour you.' But of a good leader, who talks little, when his work is done, his aim fulfilled, they will all say, 'We did this ourselves'

Lao Tzu, Chinese founder of Taoism

A leader shapes and shares a vision which gives point to the work of others

Charles Handy

Be willing to make decisions. That's the most important quality in a good leader

General George S. Patton Jr.

Leaders are individuals who establish direction for a working group of individuals who gain commitment to this direction and who then motivate these members to achieve the direction's outcomes

JA Conger

If you treat people as they are, they will stay as they are. But if you treat them as they ought to be, they will become bigger and better persons

Goethe

Leadership (according to John Sculley) revolves around vision, ideas, direction, and has more to do with inspiring people as to direction and goals than with day-to-day implementation. A leader must be able to leverage more than his own capabilities. He must be capable of inspiring other people to do things without actually sitting on top of them with a checklist

Warren Bennis

Leadership and learning are indispensable to each other

John F. Kennedy

Leadership is a combination of strategy and character. If you must be without one, be without the strategy

Gen. H. Norman Schwarzkopf

Leadership is a function of knowing yourself, having a vision that is well communicated, building trust among colleagues, and taking effective action to realize your own leadership potential

Warren Bennis

Leadership is discovering the company's destiny and having the courage to follow

Joe Jaworski

Leadership is influence – nothing more, nothing less

John Maxwell

Leadership is interpersonal influence, exercised in a situation, and directed, through the communication process, toward the attainment of a specified goal or goals

Tannenbaum, Weschler and Massarik

Leadership is not a person or a position. It is a complex moral relationship between people, based on trust, obligation, commitment, emotion and a shared vision of the good

Joanne Ciulla

Leadership is the art of mobilizing others to want to struggle for shared aspirations

J.M. Kouzes, & B.Z. 'Posner

Leadership is the capacity to translate vision into reality

Warren G. Bennis

Leadership requires using power to influence the thoughts and actions of other people

Abraham Zaleznik

Management is efficiency in climbing the ladder of success; leadership determines whether the ladder is leaning against the right wall

Stephen R. Covey

People ask the difference between a leader and a boss... The leader works in the open, and the boss in covert. The leader leads, and the boss drives

President Theodore Roosevelt

The final test of a leader is that he leaves behind in others the conviction and will to carry on

Walter Lippman

The function of leadership is to produce more leaders, not more followers

Ralph Nadar

The growth and development of people is the highest calling of leadership

Harvey S. Firestone

The key to successful leadership today is influence, not authority

Kenneth Blanchard,

The only definition of a leader is someone who has followers

The Drucker Foundation, 1996

You manage things, you lead people

Admiral Grace Murray Hooper

It is not enough to do our best. Sometimes we have to do what is required

Winston Churchill

A leader is the person in a group who directs and coordinates task-oriented group activities

F Fiedler

Leadership is a social process in which one individual influences the behaviour of others without the use of threat or violence

Buchannan and Huczynski

Leadership is about articulating visions, embodying values, and creating the environment within which things can be accomplished

Richards and Engle

*Leadership is the ability to step outside the culture to start evolution-
ary change processes that are more adaptive*

Edgar Schein

*Leadership is the lifting of a man's vision to higher sights, the raising
of a man's performance to a higher standard, the building of a man's
personality beyond its normal limitations*

Peter Drucker

*Leadership is the process of influencing the activities of an individual
or a group in efforts toward goal achievement in a given situation*

P Hersey and K Blanchard

*Leadership: the art of getting someone else to do something you want
done because he wants to do it*

President Dwight D Eisenhower

*Leadership is all hype. We've had three great leaders in this century
– Hitler, Stalin and Mao*

Peter Drucker

Other titles from Thorogood

GURUS ON PEOPLE MANAGEMENT

Sultan Kermally

£14.99 paperback, £24.99 hardback

Published March 2005

Managers HAVE to manage people. It is the most difficult and yet the most rewarding function. This book is more than just a summary of the key concepts, it offers valuable insights into their application and value including national and international real-life case studies that reflect some of the key issues of managing people.

GURUS ON BUSINESS STRATEGY

Tony Grundy

£14.99 paperback, £24.99 hardback

Published June 2003

This book is a one-stop guide to the world's most important writers on business strategy. It expertly summarises all the key strategic concepts and describes the work and contribution of each of the leading thinkers in the field.

It goes further: it analyses the pro's and con's of many of the key theories in practice and offers two enlightening case-studies. The third section of the book provides a series of detailed checklists to aid you in the development of your own strategies for different aspects of the business.

More than just a summary of the key concepts, this book offers valuable insights into their application in practice.

GURUS ON MARKETING

Sultan Kermally
£14.99 paperback, £24.99 hardback
Published November 2003

Kermally has worked directly with many of the figures in this book, including Peter Drucker, Philip Kotler and Michael Porter. It has enabled him to summarise, contrast and comment on the key concepts with knowledge, depth and insight, and to offer you fresh ideas to improve your own business. He describes the key ideas of each 'guru', places them in context and explains their significance. He shows you how they were applied in practice, looks at their pros and cons and includes the views of other expert writers.

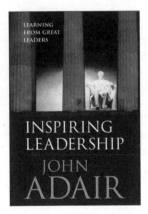

INSPIRING LEADERSHIP
Learning from great leaders

John Adair
£15.99 paperback, £24.99 hardback
Published January 2003

'I discovered once again how rare it is to come upon a book about leaders with depth, conceptual bite and historical context. It was a relief and joy'.
WARREN BENNIS, US MAJOR LEADERSHIP GURU

'I believe it is a 'must read' book... He is without doubt one of the foremost thinkers on the subject in the world.'
SIR JOHN HARVEY-JONES, PREVIOUSLY CEO OF ICI

Great leaders from Lao Tzu, Machiavelli and Washington to Thatcher, Mandela and Reagan are not only great leaders in history, they also have much to teach us today about the nature and practice of leadership. Adair uncovers their different facets of leadership in this heavily illustrated book.

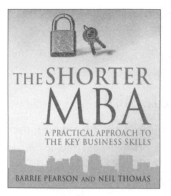

THE SHORTER MBA
A practical approach to the key business skills

Barrie Pearson and Neil Thomas
£35.00 Hardback • Published July 2004

A succinct distillation of the skills that you need to be successful in business. Most people can't afford to give up two years to study for an MBA. This pithy, practical book presents all the essential theory, practiced and techniques taught to MBA students – ideal for the busy practising executive. It is divided into three parts:

* Personal development

* Management skills

* Business development

HIGH-PERFORMANCE CONSULTING SKILLS
The internal consultant's guide to value-added performance

Mark Thomas
£14.99 paperback, £24.99 hardback
Published November 2003

This book provides a practical understanding of the skills required to become a high-performance internal consultant, whatever ones own area of expertise. It will help you to: market your services and build powerful internal networks; secure greater internal client commitment to initiatives and change projects; enhance your own worth and value to the organization; develop stronger more productive working relationships with internal clients.

BUSINESS SEMINARS

Focused on developing your potential

Falconbury, the sister company to Thorogood publishing, brings together the leading experts from all areas of management and strategic development to provide you with a comprehensive portfolio of action-centred training and learning.

We understand everything managers and leaders need to be, know and do to succeed in today's commercial environment. Each product addresses a different technical or personal development need that will encourage growth and increase your potential for success.

- Practical public training programmes
- Tailored in-company training
- Coaching
- Mentoring
- Topical business seminars
- Trainer bureau/bank
- Adair Leadership Foundation

The most valuable resource in any organization is its people; it is essential that you invest in the development of your management and leadership skills to ensure your team fulfil their potential. Investment into both personal and professional development has been proven to provide an outstanding ROI through increased productivity in both you and your team. Ultimately leading to a dramatic impact on the bottom line.

With this in mind Falconbury have developed a comprehensive portfolio of training programmes to enable managers of all levels to develop their skills in leadership, communications, finance, people management, change management and all areas vital to achieving success in today's commercial environment.

What Falconbury can offer you?

- Practical applied methodology with a proven results
- Extensive bank of experienced trainers
- Limited attendees to ensure one-to-one guidance
- Up to the minute thinking on management and leadership techniques
- Interactive training
- Balanced mix of theoretical and practical learning
- Learner-centred training
- Excellent cost/quality ratio

Falconbury In-Company Training

Falconbury are aware that a public programme may not be the solution to leadership and management issues arising in your firm. Involving only attendees from your organization and tailoring the programme to focus on the current challenges you face individually and as a business may be more appropriate. With this in mind we have brought together our most motivated and forward thinking trainers to deliver tailored in-company programmes developed specifically around the needs within your organization.

All our trainers have a practical commercial background and highly refined people skills. During the course of the programme they act as facilitator, trainer and mentor, adapting their style to ensure that each individual benefits equally from their knowledge to develop new skills.

Falconbury works with each organization to develop a programme of training that fits your needs.

Mentoring and coaching

Developing and achieving your personal objectives in the workplace is becoming increasingly difficult in today's constantly changing environment. Additionally, as a manager or leader, you are responsible for guiding colleagues towards the realization of their goals. Sometimes it is easy to lose focus on your short and long-term aims.

Falconbury's one-to-one coaching draws out individual potential by raising self-awareness and understanding, facilitating the learning and performance development that creates excellent managers and leaders. It builds renewed self-confidence and a strong sense of 'can-do' competence, contributing significant benefit to the organization. Enabling you to focus your energy on developing your potential and that of your colleagues.

Mentoring involves formulating winning strategies, setting goals, monitoring achievements and motivating the whole team whilst achieving a much improved work life balance.

Falconbury – Business Legal Seminars

Falconbury Business Legal Seminars specializes in the provision of high quality training for legal professionals from both in-house and private practice internationally.

The focus of these events is to provide comprehensive and practical training on current international legal thinking and practice in a clear and informative format.

Event subjects include, drafting commercial agreements, employment law, competition law, intellectual property, managing an in-house legal department and international acquisitions.

For more information on all our services please contact Falconbury on +44 (0)20 7729 6677 or visit the website at: www.falconbury.co.uk